CRIMINAL INVESTIGATION

CRIMINAL INVESTIGATION

EVIDENCE, CLUES, AND FORENSIC SCIENCE

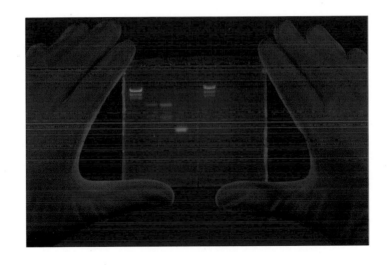

John D. Wright

Bath · New York · Singapore · Hong Kong · Cologne · Delhi · Melbourne

First published in 2008
Parragon
Queen Street House
4 Queen Street
Bath BA1 1HE, UK

Copyright © Parragon Books Ltd 2008

ISBN 978-1-4075-1772-8

Editorial and design by
Amber Books Ltd
Bradley's Close
74–77 White Lion Street
London N1 9PF
www.amberbooks.co.uk

Project Editor: James Bennett
Design: Joe Conneally
Picture Research: Kate Green

Printed in Indonesia

Picture Credits:

Contents

Introduction

"We all think of death as the ending. For forensics, it's just the beginning."

Nancy Haley, Supervisor,
Forensic Toxicology Laboratory,
Department of Health, Rhode Island

CRIME AND JUSTICE SEEMED SIMPLER IN THE EARLY NINETEENTH CENTURY BEFORE MODERN COMMUNICATIONS AND EFFICIENT TRANSPORTATION. Criminals were normally easier to apprehend because they lived in small communities with their victims and any eyewitnesses—the hit-and-run crime would have to wait for a modern infrastructure. And when suspects were arrested and tried, convictions were normally based on public opinion and even resulted from pressures put on the defendant, including torture. This easy justice, however, was often injustice in the years before standard police procedures and scientific evaluations of evidence.

Today's criminals use modern technology, including emails, cellphone messages, and even television appearances. Ian Huntley, who murdered two ten-year-old girls in Soham, Cambridgeshire, England, was soon on a BBC news program coolly speaking about the community's shock. However, the investigative tools of forensic science have also advanced at a remarkable pace. Infrared spectrometers identify fibers left by suspects, CT scanners pinpoint weapons in suitcases, and DNA solves "cold cases" that are decades old. Introduced in the 1980s, DNA testing has been recently refined to obtain results from only a few cells, ten times fewer than conventional DNA testing.

EVERY CONTACT LEAVES A TRACE

To the trained eye, a crime scene is filled with clues that can be obvious or mysterious. They involve physical evidence like fingerprints, hair, blood, fibers, drugs, paint, or soil. Arthur Conan Doyle's fictional detective Sherlock Holmes, who first appeared in 1887, emphasized the importance of miniscule evidence. He searched for fingerprints, analyzed blood and examined documents. The idea that "every contact leaves a trace" was stated in 1920 by Dr. Edmond Locard, a French police officer and forensic scientist who 10 years earlier had established the world's first crime laboratory in Lyon, France. His concept, now known as Locard's Exchange Principle, is the key to

Left: A forensic scientist collects fiber samples for microscopic examination as part of a criminal investigation. Fibers from clothing and carpets are among the most common items of trace evidence that are recovered.

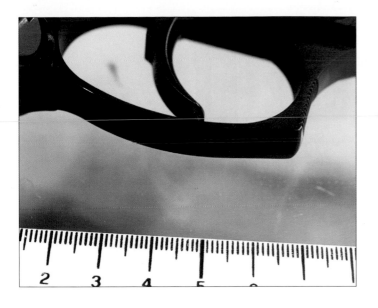

Above: Forensic scientist checks for fingerprints on a bottle at a crime scene. His protective suit prevents contamination of the evidence.

modern forensic science. In practice this means physical evidence will be exchanged during any physical contact between a suspect and his victim or the crime scene. A criminal might leave his fingerprints or a hair at the scene, and take away carpet fabric on his shoes.

Such evidence is carefully collected and turned over to forensic scientists who handle such diverse crimes as identity theft, kidnapping, burglary, arson, rape, and murder. If someone has died, forensic pathologists calculate the time and cause of death and a nameless victim can be identified by a variety of methods, which include fingerprints, a dental match, and facial reconstruction in clay or by computer.

The forensic laboratory is often the key to a successful police investigation. The lab results should indicate if a crime was committed and, if so, tests can verify evidence that helps convict the person or persons responsible. Placing a suspect at the crime scene is a basic goal of forensic work. That connection is often a clear sign of guilt, as when fresh tire marks are found at the scene of an arson attack.

EVIDENCE IN COURT

The name "forensic science" means science related to crime and courts of law. The word "forensic" goes back to the Latin *forum* where legal matters were settled. Forensic experts, indeed, are called to testify in court cases by both the prosecution and the defense. The

trail from a crime scene to a courtroom has a sequence that is well established, which can involve specialists in several forensic fields working closely with law enforcement officers. The scientific tools and techniques they use are impressive, but lab results have to be evaluated by highly trained professionals possessing knowledge, experience, and intuition.

The following chapters will look at how evidence is collected at crime scenes, the ways of determining the time and cause of death, of identifying unknown victims and suspects, what tools and tests are used in the modern forensic laboratory, the way DNA profiling has revolutionized the fight against crime, how forensic scientists solve white-collar crimes, and what drives a criminal mind.

Left: A blood sample is shown on a microscope slide. A forensic serologist will use it for DNA profiling to try to establish a link between a suspect's blood and that found at the crime scene.

Forensic Evidence

A crime cannot be solved without evidence of some sort. Confessions and circumstantial evidence sometimes prove untrue, but physical evidence can provide an airtight case against a suspect.

Guilty verdicts have been achieved by an expert's testimony involving a single hair or piece of fiber. For this reason, a forensic scientist's primary focus at a crime scene is to discover these small pieces known as "trace evidence," with other examples including skin, gunshot residue, and dust.

Fingerprints are sometimes described as trace evidence, as well as the prints of palms and soles at the crime scene. Fingerprints can be removed to be compared to those already on file in a database or to prints taken from suspects. They are also valuable in identifying an unknown victim. Prints made by shoes, gloves, and tires are also useful. In addition, investigators search for marks left by tools such as those used for breaking into a house.

FIREARMS

If a firearm has been deployed in a crime and recovered, forensic scientists will use chemicals and microscopes to examine the gun and its projectiles. Strong evidence is provided when bullets or shell casings are matched to the firearm of a suspect.

DOCUMENTS

In a variety of criminal cases, a document examiner provides another type of forensic identification. This involves written evidence such as a kidnapper's note, an altered will, account book, or lottery ticket, as well as a forged signature on a check or a forged passport. Besides analyzing the handwriting, a document expert may be called upon to determine the age and source of the paper and ink.

Of course, evidence can be found away from the primary crime scene. This is why careful searches are made of a suspect's home and vehicle, as well as sites associated with the victim.

Numbered crime scene markers are used to indicate the position of every item of relevance such as this discarded gun. Each position is logged before the evidence is removed for analysis in a forensic laboratory.

If a firearm has been deployed in a crime and recovered, forensic scientists will use chemicals and microscopes to examine the gun and its projectiles.

Protective clothing assures this cartridge shell will pass as court evidence.

EVIDENCE CONTAMINATION

Once evidence is found, it must be photographed in its original position and placed in separate bags or containers that are clearly labeled. These are transported to a forensic laboratory for examination and later may be presented as exhibits in court. All this must be done without contaminating the items. This can happen, for instance, if a fiber from an investigator's clothes is transferred onto the victim's clothes or if the evidential object is dropped on the lab floor. Any hint of contamination will normally make evidence inadmissible in court. The best way to avoid complications is a "chain of custody" for those who handle the evidence—the fewer the better—by keeping a documented "continuity of evidence" record of its movement.

National Forensic Services

The developed nations of the world have established modern and efficient forensic science services that have had remarkable success in working together on international cases.

In the United States, the Federal Bureau of Investigation (FBI) Laboratory in Washington, D.C., was established in 1932 as the Technical Laboratory. It now has a Combined DNA Index System (CODIS), which is a national computerized database available to the 50 individual states, all of whom have their own DNA databases of convicted offenders. The laboratory also runs a Forensic Science Research and Training Center in Quantico, Virginia.

The Royal Canadian Mounted Police (RCMP) has the Forensic Laboratory Services as part of its National Police Services in Ottawa where the National DNA Data Bank is located. The RCMP's forensic laboratories are in Vancouver,

J. Edgar Hoover F.B.I. Building

Left: Former British Prime Minister Tony Blair looks into a microscope during his visit in 2006 to the Forensic Science Service headquarters in London.

Below: A scene of crime officer (SOCO) adds labels to collection tubes. These hold swabs containing saliva samples that are used to recover DNA.

Edmonton, Regina, Winnipeg, Ottawa, and Halifax, while Ontario and Quebec have their own labs.

The United Kingdom has the Forensic Science Service (FSS) within the Home Office where it was created in 1991 from regional forensic laboratories. It now oversees those six labs in London, Birmingham, Chepstow, Huntingdon, Chorley, and Wetherby. The National Firearms Unit (NFU) is in Manchester. There is also a Forensic Science Agency of Northern Ireland and four labs in Scotland for the areas of Grampian, Strathclyde, Tayside, and Lothian and Borders.

Private companies also offer forensic laboratory examinations and are often employed in court cases by defense and prosecution teams. The U.K.'s largest, LGC, is headquartered in Teddington, Middlesex and has more than 1,000 employees. More than 150 years old, it was the Laboratory of the Government Chemist before being privatized in 1996. In 2005 it acquired Forensic Alliance Limited (FAL), then the U.K.'s largest private sector provider of forensic science services. The newly combined group has five laboratories about the country and a specialist firearms facility.

EUROPEAN FORENSICS

Criminal justice in the twenty-first century has to deal with perpetrators who can communicate worldwide in an instant and, especially in Europe, move effortlessly across country borders. To combat this, national agencies of law enforcement and forensic science work closely together, sharing the latest science and technology. The European Network of Forensic Science Institutes (ENFSI) promotes cooperation between the forensic laboratories from 32 European countries.

A leading provider is the U.K.'s Forensic Science Service (FSS), which has assisted more than 60 countries. The first organization in the world that developed a national criminal DNA database, its expertise is available to forensic facilities, police forces, and government organizations around the world. The service also sends experts to different countries to train forensic scientists in their own laboratories.

The FSS maintains the world's most extensive database containing abstracts of forensic science literature, with more than 70,000 records. This covers problems encountered in analytical laboratories and such various topics as DNA, computer crime, documents examination, and arson investigation.

Types of Forensic Specialties

Forensic science is a broad practice that embraces science used for legal purposes, and its practitioners range from physicians to laboratory assistants.

Their specialty may deal with human remains such as cadavers, bones, hair, and teeth or with inanimate evidence such as fingerprints, firearms, detonators, wills, and checks. Some of the major specialties, which may include subspecialties, are:

FORENSIC PATHOLOGY:

This involves autopsies by licensed physicians of bodies that have not yet decomposed. This postmortem examination of the external and internal parts of the deceased is done to establish the cause and time of death. If murder seems evident, the pathologist often visits the crime scene to view the position of the victim. Living victims are also examined in such cases as assault and rape to determine injuries and their causes.

FORENSIC ANTHROPOLOGY:

This is concerned with postmortem examinations of the remains of human bones, usually to identify the deceased and hopefully establish the cause and time of death. This study can determine the age, sex, height, and race of a victim, as well as injuries and illnesses.

FORENSIC ODONTOLOGY:

This specializes in the examination of teeth, which are the hardest and most durable substance in the body. When a corpse is badly decomposed, therefore, the best means of identification is often by matching the victim's teeth with dental records. Odontologists also compare a suspect's teeth with bite marks on a victim or on food left at the crime scene.

FORENSIC TOXICOLOGY:

This is the scientific study of poisons and drugs used in murders and other criminal cases such as date-rape drugs. Tests are also run on the living to determine if such substances caused them to act violently or drive dangerously.

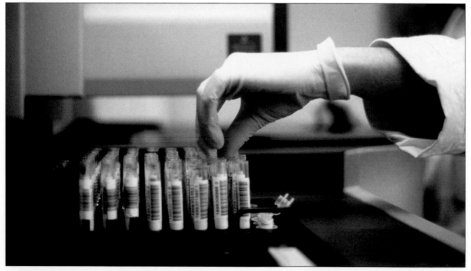

A laboratory technician in France selects a blood sample for testing. The samples are carefully kept in bar-coded tubes to assure the correct identifications.

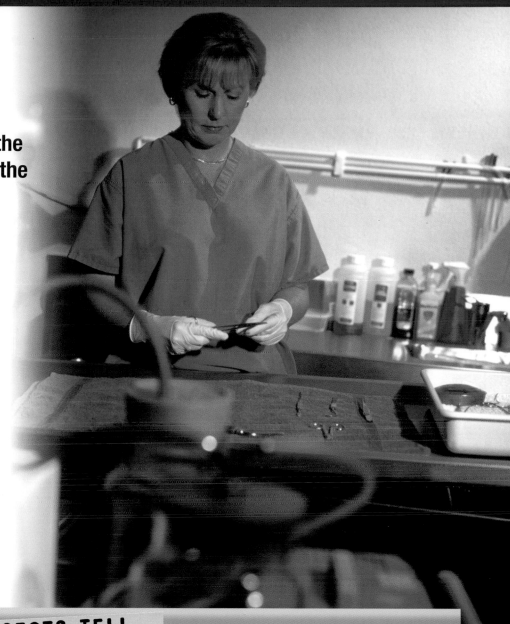

If murder seems evident, the pathologist will often visit the crime scene.

FORENSIC SEROLOGY:

This is the field that examines blood and other bodily fluids such as saliva and semen. Among the serologist's tests are blood typing and DNA profiling.

FORENSIC ENTOMOLOGY:

This concerns the study of flies and other insects on a corpse, since their known life cycles can be used to estimate a victim's time of death.

WHAT FLIES AND INSECTS TELL

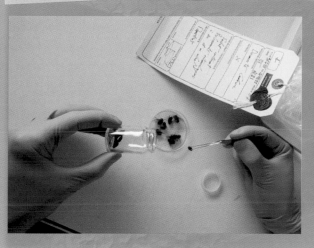

A forensic entomologist uses a technique that dates back to about the thirteenth century in China. It was known then that looking at the stages of development and sizes of insect larvae on a body could establish the time of death. Tests on their larvae can also reveal a poison, because they take poison up from human tissue. This is important for toxicological tests because body fluids and soft tissues are soon gone from a corpse. The type of insects can also indicate a body was moved from the insects' natural habitat, since some flies prefer laying eggs indoors or outdoors and others always choose shade or sunlight. The concentration of insects on a part of the body may show where wounds are located.

Preventing Contamination

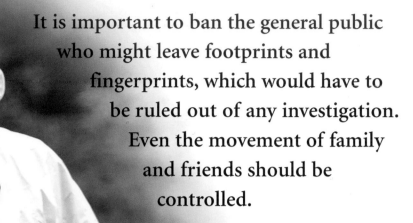

It is important to ban the general public who might leave footprints and fingerprints, which would have to be ruled out of any investigation. Even the movement of family and friends should be controlled.

Controlling the scene is especially difficult when a crime is committed in a public urban setting. This was the case when the controversial Dutch filmmaker, Theo Van Gogh, was murdered in 2004 by an Islamic extremist on an Amsterdam street, and occurred on a greater scale with the terrorist bombings of transportation systems in Madrid in 2004 and London the following year. In such cases busy public areas must be sealed off and made secure, often for several days.

PROTECTIVE UNIFORM

Investigators allowed onto a crime scene have to be sensitive to the danger of cross-contamination. They should wear a white protective uniform that

HOW INSPECTORS CONTAMINATE SCENES

A recurrent problem with contaminated evidence at crime scenes involves inspectors leaving their own trace evidence, including DNA, at the scene and even on the victim. Many unidentified profiles in DNA databases that were thought to belong to perpetrators have proven to be from officers on the scene.

In a 2003 murder case in New South Wales, Australia, an unknown DNA profile was found on the victim's jumper that did not match the suspect. Then in 2005, the same DNA profile was found after a violent armed robbery. When police who handled both cases were examined, the DNA was matched to a forensic services investigator.

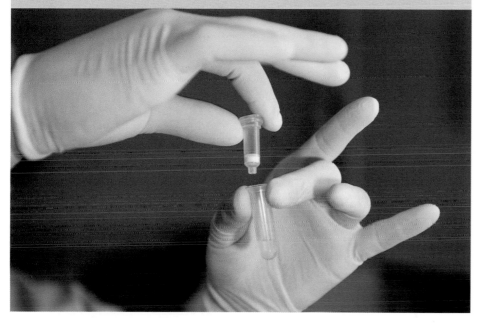

JONBENET RAMSEY

Sympathetic officers are sometimes lenient when confronted with distressed family members. This happened after the murder of 6-year-old JonBenet Ramsey in 1996 in Boulder, Colorado. Her father discovered the body in the basement, and police allowed him to carry it upstairs. They also permitted friends to move freely in the house. The evidence was therefore badly compromised, and the case remains unsolved.

The laboratory work on the JonBenet Ramsey murder case included an intense examination of a ransom note, but its author was never identified.

includes a mask, surgical gloves, and plastic overshoes. If officials need to pass through part of the scene to reach the focal point such as a victim, a common approach path will be designated to protect any evidence. A homicide victim and normal objects should not be touched or moved before the forensic scientist arrives. The position of a door or window, for example, could be crucial to solving a case. Officials should also stop anyone else from changing the scene, as when a crime survivor or family members try to put a room back in order.

If more than one crime scene exists for a case such as a victim being murdered at one location and buried at another, a forensic scientist must try to avoid covering both scenes and risking cross-contamination. If only one person is available to examine both areas, he or she should undergo decontamination before switching sites.

Securing the Scene

Onlookers are drawn to tragedies, such as when a building is on fire, vehicles collide, or miners are trapped underground. The news media will also rapidly converge on such a site.

Public curiosity can create difficulties, and it becomes a significant problem when a murder or other major crime has been committed. Officials needed to sort out the situation will already occupy the scene. This may include police, forensic scientists, firemen, physicians, ambulance personnel, and possibly more specialists, such as bomb disposal experts.

The size of a crime scene can be limited to one room or spread over an extensive area, as happened when more than 1,000 police and soldiers had to search 845 sq miles/2,189 sq km of Scottish countryside in 1988 after a Pan American flight was bombed over the village of Lockerbie, killing 270 people.

FIRST OFFICER ATTENDING

The immediate job for the first policeman on the scene, known as the first officer attending (FOA), is to help any victims who are alive. If they are injured, medical treatment

NICOLE SIMPSON AND RONALD GOLDMAN

The murder trial of footballer and actor O. J. Simpson involved the stabbings of his former wife, Nicole Simpson, and her friend, Ronald Goldman. It was a small crime scene: just the walkway leading to her apartment. The first two officers on the scene determined that the victims were dead and, with three more officers, they secured the scene, created a sign-in sheet and, by the time two detectives arrived, there were already 18 officers present. A police photographer joined them but could only take area shots until the civilian forensic scientist arrived.

Detectives then went to O. J. Simpson's house, declaring it too a crime scene. From there the police criminalist collected blood spots and a bloody glove. Despite this and other evidence, Simpson was acquitted in 1995 after a televised trial that lasted more than eight months.

is the immediate concern, even if this destroys evidence. A victim's general condition should not be cleaned, however, until a forensic officer has checked for bloodstains, hair, and other trace evidence.

The first authorities will also detain any possible suspects and eyewitnesses, taking down their statements. They should be kept separate to avoid having trace evidence transferred from one person to another. If someone had reported the crime, they should be interviewed, detained and denied access to the crime scene. Perpetrators have been known to report their crime to appear innocent and gain entry in order to confuse the scene. A crime area should also be sealed off from onlookers to prevent evidence from being contaminated or lost. The police will cordon off the site, normally marking the perimeter with tape, and will restrict the areas of access, logging in all visitors and recording what they remove. Tents may be erected to protect the scene from the elements and onlookers.

Above: Scene of crime officers (SOCOs) investigate a shooting. Police tape marks out the boundaries of the crime scene. The SOCOs are wearing paper suits, overshoes, and masks to prevent contamination of evidence.

Below: Wreckage of the bombed Pan American airline lies on Scottish soil after 270 lives were lost.

Suspects and witnesses should all be kept separate to avoid trace evidence being transferred from one person to another.

Recording the Evidence

Sketches, oral tapes, videotapes, and notes are taken at a crime scene. A police or forensic photographer, however, who records the overall view, including the surrounding area and small evidential details, does the best documentation.

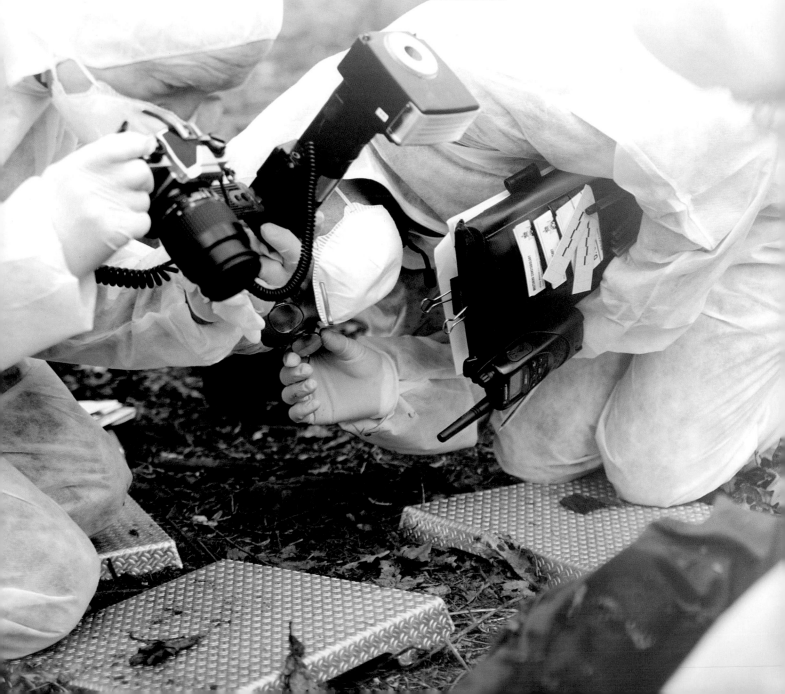

An item of evidence is filmed next to a ruler to indicate the size and again alone, in case the ruler had covered more evidence. Other references can be used in the photo to indicate size such as a pen or coin.

The photographer is usually one of the first allowed through the site, since the undisturbed scene must be recorded before victims are taken to the morgue or hospital and objects are removed to forensic laboratories. Photos also record fragile evidence such as latent fingerprints that may be ruined during their recovery and evidence that may alter over time such as a cigarette stub. Close-up images will be taken of wounds on a corpse or injured person. After a body has been removed, photos should be taken of the area where it lay.

Recording the scene by video has the advantage of adding comments, but still photographs present the sharpest images and are the easiest to handle in a courtroom.

Each shot is labeled with a number, the location of the scene, the date and time taken, and information about the processing.

WHY TAKE NOTES?

Notes are valuable because they can record the sequence of actions taken by officials, whose names and titles are listed with the times they were at the scene. A written description has the advantage of recording changes at the scene during the investigation. Lists can record several facts about each item of evidence: the object and its description, when and where it was discovered, and by whom. One list can serve as a log of photographs taken, describing them, their location, when and where they were taken, and the name of the camera operator.

All this must stand up in court when a clever attorney raises the doubt that someone may have tampered with the prints during the process.

DIGITAL CAMERAS

The advent of digital cameras has introduced the ability to enhance images. This type of camera can remove the background confusion if fingerprints are blurred when overlapping a patterned background, as found on a stamp, bank note or ticket. Such a change, however, carries the suggestion of manipulation, and some juries may discount the value of that evidence.

SKETCHY EVIDENCE?

Sketching is still used to indicate spatial relationship at a crime scene between objects or with an object and a corpse. Sketches are particularly clear, because unimportant items will not be shown and wounds on a body can be emphasized. Sometimes sketches are the only record available of the undisturbed crime scene, if a body has to be removed before the photographer arrives.

Finding Evidence

A crime scene needs to be searched quickly and thoroughly. If evidence remains after police remove their security restrictions, it will be compromised and unusable.

Most sites remain sealed off for a day or more, but this can vary according to the crime: in Canada police barred entrance to the international wing of Jean-Lesage Airport in 2007 in Quebec City for three hours after a false X-ray alarm, while the street in a Vienna suburb where Natascha Kampusch escaped after eight years of captivity in 2006 was closed for several days.

Investigators use their experience and common sense when probing through a site for clues. The crime-scene manager and scene of crime officers (SOCOs) will be trained in forensics. The police collecting evidence wear protective kits. They may advance in a line across an outdoor area or crawl along an indoor scene shoulder-to-shoulder conducting a fingertip search. A geometric search pattern may follow a spiral route

DR. DAVID KELLY

An example of high standards in a crime-scene search involved the death of Dr. David Kelly, an employee of the UK Ministry of Defence, who committed suicide in 2003 after being named as the source criticizing the British government's statement on weapons of mass destruction in Iraq.

When his body was discovered in a wood, a Home Office pathologist and forensic biologists looked at the scene. Police teams conducted a thorough four-hour fingertip search 33 ft/10 m on either side of the scene's approach path they had established and also searched a

radius of 33 ft/10 m around Dr. Kelly's body. It was then removed and a 30-minute search was made of the ground where it had been. Nothing of significance was found.

toward or from a corpse, while large areas can be divided into quadrants to be searched in a straight line or a criss-cross grid pattern.

If evidence might be both outside and inside a building, the former is searched first due to the possibility of rain and wind ruining the items. The search will also concentrate on the criminal's probable entry and exit paths.

FINDING EVIDENCE IN ISRAEL

In Israel the criminal identification technician (CDT) is responsible for finding the physical evidence at a crime scene, as a complement to an investigator's work. In this initial examination, field kits are used to seek evidence such as fingerprints, footprints, and bloodstains. The CDT also documents the scene of the crime with photographs and drawings. The technician then transfers the evidence to laboratories located at the national facility in Jerusalem for tests. On some occasions, the CDT is asked to testify in court about the evidence found at the scene and to provide expert opinions submitted to the court as evidence.

Right: Israeli forensic experts examine the scene of a suicide bombing that killed eight people in Tel Aviv in April 2006.

Collecting Evidence

First, evidence that is fragile or in danger of contamination such as fibers and hair must be attended to. This trace evidence can be collected from areas such as carpets and floors, furniture, and car seats, using a special vacuum, tweezers, clear tape, or by hand.

Clothes and other textile products can be simply shaken or brushed to recover hairs. In all cases wearing surgical gloves will avoid any transference of an investigator's DNA to the evidence.

Fingerprints are among the best evidence that can be recovered. They are a personal signature, and have been accepted in court cases for more than a century.

Argentina saw the first person convicted of murder by the use of fingerprints, Francisca Rohas, who killed her two sons in 1892 and cut her own throat trying to blame the crime on an attacker who had broken in.

Visible prints are classified as either patent prints, such as those stained with blood, grease, and paint; or as plastic prints, which are impressions in some soft material such as putty, soap, and dust.

Others indicators of a suspect's presence at a crime scene are footprints and tire tracks. If both are left in soft ground, they can be photographed, cast in plaster, lifted, and then compared with known shoes and tires belonging to a suspect. If shoe prints are found on a floor or other hard surface, they can be detected the same way as fingerprints are, by applying a powder. Such shoe marks can be lifted by a fabric covered with a sticky gel or by an electrostatic device.

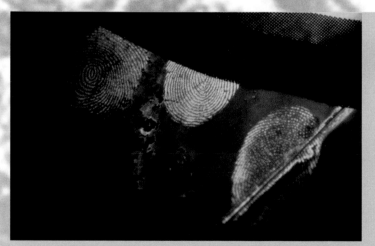

Fingerprints on a scarf are revealed here using a laser technique. The fingerprints are dusted with a chemical that fluoresces when exposed to laser light. This technique is useful because it works on porous surfaces.

LATENT FINGERPRINTS

Latent prints, which are invisible, are still detectable because light can reveal any sweat or oil on a surface left behind by fingers. When an angled beam of ultraviolet light, or a laser, is shone over the prints they will fluoresce, or glow. Latent prints can also be made visible by applying a powder, often carbon black, white, or gray aluminum to the prints, using a soft brush. If marks have been absorbed on porous surfaces such as paper, magnetic powder can be applied by an applicator that does not touch the surface. All prints are then carefully lifted by a transparent tape and mounted.

Scales are placed over a can of soda to be photographed at a crime scene. The can has been dusted for fingerprints.

GENERAL-PURPOSE SCIENTIFIC TOOLS

- **Exposing evidence:** magnifying glass, flashlight, and laser, infrared, and ultraviolet lights

- **Recovering prints:** aluminum and black powders, black and gray magnetic powders, soft brush, magnetic applicator, gel fingerprint and footprint lifters, clear lifting tape, white latent print cards

- **Collecting trace evidence such as hairs, fibers, and fluids:** tweezers, utility knife, scissors, and cotton swabs

- **Making casts of tires, footprints and tool marks:** casting plaster, mixing bowl, and spatula

- **Packaging evidence:** permanent pen, evidence labels, plastic and paper bags, and glass tubes

Forensic researchers wear special glasses to see the faint glow of fingerprints (shown in green) that are triggered by a flashing fluorescent lamp.

Reconstructing the Crime

A primary goal of police and forensic investigators at a crime scene is to reconstruct the crime—determining what the crime was, the sequence of events, who was present, their positions and actions.

This involves getting a feel for the scene and the evidence, interviewing any witnesses, suspects, and surviving victims, and then using scientific methods and logical reasoning. Criminal profiling will be added to understand why the crime happened and what this reveals about who may have done it.

RECONSTRUCTIVE EVIDENCE

Clues as to what happened are known as reconstructive evidence. The direction of shoe prints, fingerprints, or tool marks on a window or door, the position of blood splatters and bullet trajectories, and the victim's wounds, which can indicate the positions of the attacker and victim, can all be used to piece together the crime.

A deceased individual slumped in a dining-room chair with a wound to his temple and a gun resting on the floor below his outstretched arm may seem to be a clear case of suicide. However, an examination uncovers wounds to the back of his head, scuff marks indicating a struggle, and traces of skin under the victim's fingernails. Therefore, the original assumption of suicide quickly changes into a murder investigation. No fingerprints are uncovered on the gun but latent prints are on the door of a cabinet containing silver pieces. Investigators propose their theory: the victim surprised a burglar intent on stealing the silver. They struggled until the assailant struck the victim down, shot him, and arranged the suicide scene, having to leave the silver behind.

This is an example of a staged crime scene, where the perpetrator leaves false clues to mislead

Forensic investigators can calculate bullet trajectories by creating a three-dimensional computer reconstruction of a crime scene.

RECONSTRUCTION CLUES

When retired Group Captain T. P. Singh, his wife, Shibani, and sister, Ajit Kaur were murdered together in 2006 in Chandigarh, India, forensic experts helped police reconstruct the crime. Tracks showed that the perpetrator killed the man, followed by his wife and sister, which indicated one or a few assailants. The wife had thrown a flower vase at the assailant(s) and her hair had been pulled, indicating she had fought back. Two gunshots were found in the man's body, showing he had tried to escape. His sister was hit on the head, so she was caught unawares. Four blood types were collected, and the case is ongoing.

investigators. Such cases could also include a husband killing his wife with several blows and then positioning her body at the bottom of the stairs to indicate an accident, an arsonist who sets a fire to consume the body of a murder victim, or a person involved in insurance fraud, hiding her own jewelry and staging a burglary by scattering contents from drawers and breaking a window.

The BBC "Crimewatch" program reenacts (above) the stabbing of Abigail Witchalls in Surrey, England, in 2005, and a gendarme (left) checks a dummy used to recreate the 1999 murder of Isabel Peake in France.

Checking for Life

When a body is discovered, the priority is to check for vital signs such as a pulse, heartbeat, and breathing. A medical examiner will use a stethoscope to attempt to find a faint heartbeat.

A CORONER AT THE SCENE

Disagreement exists on whether a coroner is actually needed at a crime scene, because some believe a coroner hinders the work. During the inquiry into Dr. Harold Shipman's murders, the forensic pathologist Dr. Peter Acland said a coroner at the scene of death could contaminate evidence and make decisions that complicate the investigation. Dr. Acland added that he had never known the involvement of a coroner to benefit a crime-scene investigation. Michael Burgess, representing the Coroners' Society, added that he saw potential problems with a coroner being physically present at the death scene. However, he said that a coroner or someone separate from the police should be there with the power to authorize an autopsy of the body.

Any slightest indication of life calls for resuscitation or other critical medical treatment, and this takes priority over the arrest of a suspect and the possible contamination of evidence. This has been obvious during terrorist attacks such as the Madrid bombings of March 11, 2004.

Badly injured victims can seem lifeless, so great care must be taken in examining a body for life. When a man brutally attacked Dr. Lin Russell and her two daughters, Megan and Josie, with a hammer in 1996 on an isolated lane near Canterbury, Kent, England, one of the two police officers first on the scene, Constable Richard Leivers, checked for signs of life and found none. Dr. Shaun Russell, the husband and father, was told of the discovery and informed that all of his family had died. However, as the police surgeon, Dr. Michael Parks, arrived at the murder scene, Constable Leivers noticed that the body of nine-year-old Josie moved.

"I had ascertained that the female adult was cold and had

Michael Stone, arriving at the High Court in London on January 18, 2005, was found guilty of murder.

no signs of life,' Dr. Parks reported. "I immediately diverted my attentions to the child. She moved when I touched her and felt warm. I reassured her and after a brief period of reflection I asked PC Leivers to pick her up. She was semi-conscious and had clear head injuries."

The girl had lain barely alive next to the bodies of her mother and sister for an hour. Although she suffered severe head injuries, Josie made an amazing recovery. Her taped interview by police was presented as evidence at the trial of Michael Stone, who was convicted of the murders in 1998 and given three life sentences.

Resuscitation or other critical medical treatment takes priority over the possible contamination of evidence.

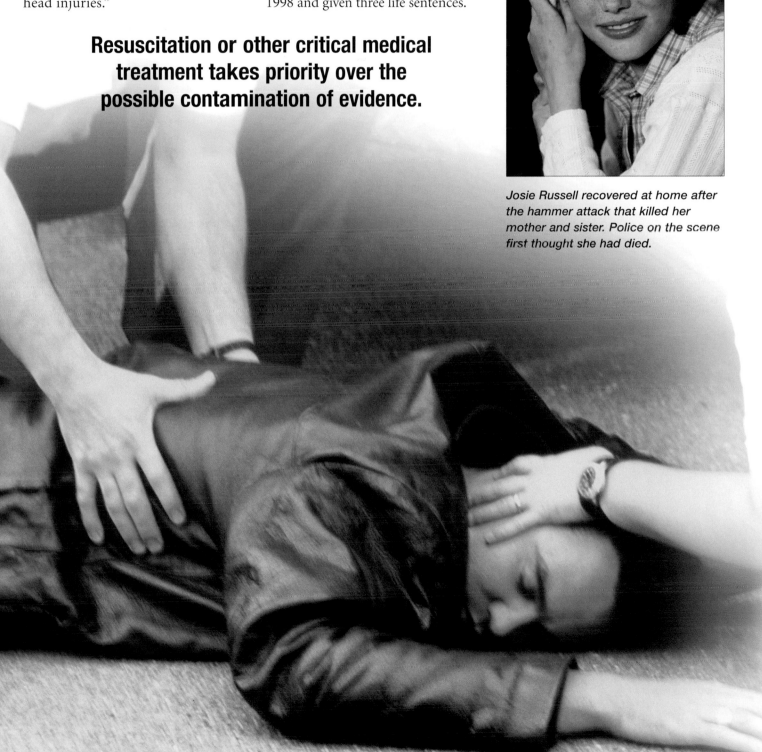

Josie Russell recovered at home after the hammer attack that killed her mother and sister. Police on the scene first thought she had died.

Examining a Body at the Scene

A forensic pathologist examines a body found at a possible crime scene before it is removed to the morgue. The first examination may be done with the corpse *in situ*, or it may have to be moved for a proper examination.

This is why its original undisturbed position of the body is first photographed, videotaped, or sketched.

The pathologist carries only a notepad and pen to the scene, but the crime scene manager or medical examiner provides any other necessary items such as a thermometer, swabs for the removal of a sample of any fluids or marks on the body or clothes, and containers for storing evidence.

The examination will concentrate on determining the time of death, since this may be a vital clue in linking the murder to a suspect. The time of death, never an exact figure, will be more difficult to judge after the body is removed, an action that will also eliminate signs of rigor mortis.

It may be necessary to remove the deceased's clothing to check for discoloration of the skin. A dead person's skin in the lower regions begins to take on a pink-red color, or lividity, due to blood settling. This begins some 30 minutes to 2 hours after death and is complete by 8 to 12 hours. This is caused by gravity, so a corpse lying on its left side has lividity on its left shoulder, arm, hip, and leg. The overall skin also takes on a greenish tint after 48 hours because of bacteria. This becomes a marbled look after four to seven days. Dark skin, however, will not show these colors.

The temperature of the cadaver is measured with a rectal thermometer. After death, the temperature of the body's trunk will generally fall about 1.5°F/ 0.8°C for each hour.

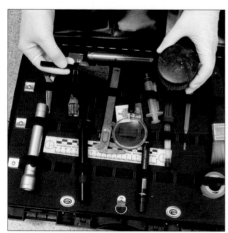

A forensic investigator, gloved to avoid contamination, removes a container of fine powder from a crime scene kit for fingerprint work.

CADAVERIC SPASM

Sometimes a corpse will have a kind of instant rigor mortis called "cadaveric spasm." This happens when the muscles were being used with great exertion while dying, as during a struggle or while running hard. This is why the victim might have a death grip on a weapon. A cadaveric spasm, of course, can add confusion to the time of death.

RIGOR MORTIS

A pathologist at the crime scene will check for this stiffening of the body by carefully trying to move the arms and legs, neck, jaw, and eyelids. Rigor mortis normally occurs from 30 minutes to 3 hours after death, taking hold first in the eyelids, jaw and neck, then progressing downward. The whole body is affected within 8 to 12 hours, the stiffness continues for up to 18 hours, and is gone after a further 6 to 12 hours. Sometimes at low temperatures, rigor mortis will not even be present.

It is extremely important for a pathologist to investigate the body of a crime victim as soon as possible after discovery. By the time a body reaches the morgue, vital information will have been lost.

A forensic researcher examines a carbonized corpse in a burnt-out apartment in order to determine the fire's cause and the corpse's identity.

Signs of Violence

Although conclusive proof of a violent crime can be obtained in a forensic laboratory, a forensic pathologist will make a careful examination of a corpse at the scene of death.

Below: This three-dimensional CT scan shows the fractured skull of a man involved in an assault. Direct brain damage and even death can result from such injuries.

Obvious signs include wounds made by gunshot and by blunt and sharp instruments. Cutting, stabbing, and puncture marks are examples of defensive wounds that are normally found on the back of the victim's hands, inside the palms, and the inner side of the forearms. Scrapes and bruises can also suggest a struggle.

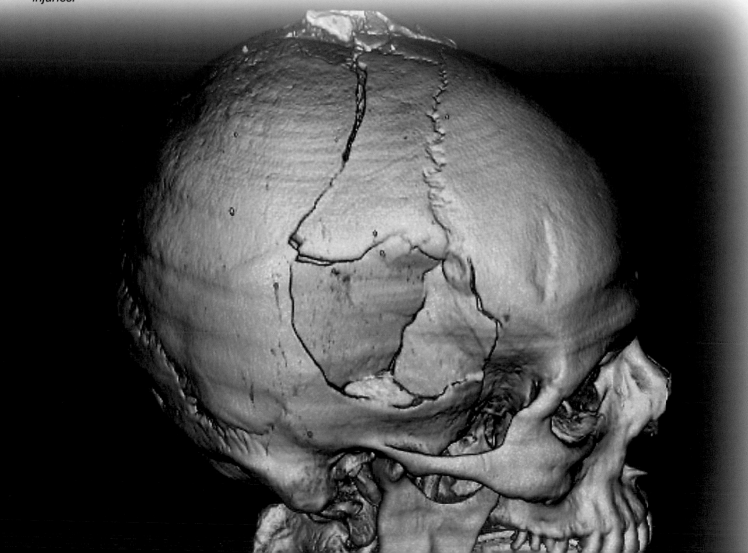

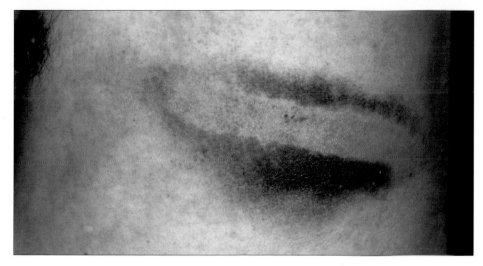

Bruising such as this could be the result of a beating with a club or baseball bat, and will be investigated carefully by a pathologist.

Violent marks on the body can also disprove an apparent suicide or accident victim. When the wife of a traffic policeman was found dead in front of her house in Cholurpalya, India, in 2004, it was ruled she committed suicide jumping from the balcony. However, a postmortem report found she had been strangled, and police arrested her husband and his father.

Other marks indicating violence include those made by ropes, tapes, bandages, or other devices used to bind a victim, marks of a blindfold or gag, and those associated with torture such as cigarette burns.

In some cases, despite having obvious marks and trauma, victims may deny they were assaulted, either to protect the perpetrator such as a spouse or out of fear of further violence. Police violence can be especially intimidating. The Asian Human Rights Commission has highlighted this such as the case of R. Don Nawaratne Bandara of Panadura, Sri Lanka. They say he was severely tortured by police in 2001 but withdrew his case against them because he feared for his life. The UN International Criminal Tribunal for the Former Yugoslavia also encountered many victims who refused to testify, citing their own safety. Its first case was dropped after a woman withdrew a rape charge because she could not be anonymous.

TYPES OF WOUNDS

Forensic examiners encounter many different types of wounds, or lesions, and traumas caused by physical assault.

Some of the common type of injury are:

Abrasion: an injury in which the skin is scraped off

Concussion: a serious brain injury caused by a hard blow to the head

Contusion: a bruise in which the skin is not broken

Fracture: a break, crack, or shattering of a bone

Laceration: a cut that is deep enough to need stitches

Trauma: a wound or a physical or emotional shock to the body

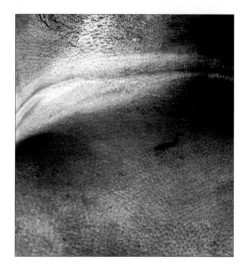

A murder victim has strangulation marks on the back of his neck caused by a thick cord. The appearance of the skin helps determine the time of death.

A LACK OF MARKS

Just the indication of overturned objects is sometimes enough to indicate foul play. When police in Hawaii discovered the body of a 40-year-old woman in 2000, there were no apparent physical marks of violence on her body but the nearby scene indicated a struggle, so they tentatively classified her death as a homicide. This initiated an immediate investigation that led to an arrest.

The Forensic Laboratory

In a large forensic crime lab, white-coated scientists and technicians bend over an array of complicated instruments, some scan computer screens, while others handle hazardous specimens using glove-boxes.

The object of all this lab activity is to verify that a crime has been committed and to connect criminal evidence to a suspect. This normally requires close cooperation between basic local police labs and larger regional and national ones where separate departments exist for each specialty. Britain's Forensic Science Service, for example, works primarily for the 43 police forces in England and Wales.

In 2007 it launched its new Footwear Intelligence Technology System accessible to all police forces and containing some 13,000 images of shoe-print types most commonly found at crime scenes.

ASSESSING A SAMPLE

Lab work often begins with a scientist briefly assessing a collected sample to identify it and determine if more expensive tests are required. Expertise will help decide if a stain is blood, a metal fragment comes from a bomb or if a hair is human or animal. Samples are then sent to specialized divisions for testing and analysis. In Canada's Forensic Science Services, departments exist for biology, chemistry, explosives, toxicology, firearms and trace evidence, and there is also a bureau for counterfeit and document examinations. The evidence will be physically handled by scientists and their lab assistants such as analysts and technicians. To avoid evidence contamination every sample is stored and logged to follow its progress through the various departments.

FORENSIC PIONEERS

Edmond Locard (1877–1966) established the world's first forensic laboratory in Lyon, France, in 1910. He had been an assistant to the famed physician Alexandre Lacassagne (below), who was himself called "the father of forensic science." Locard was famous for his idea that "every contact leaves a trace," now known as the Locard Exchange Principle. Two years after opening his crime lab, Locard used it to solve a case in which a bank clerk murdered his girlfriend. The man seemed to have a perfect alibi but confessed after Locard found minute scrapings of skin under his fingernails containing the pink dust of the woman's face powder.

Students receive first-aid instruction at the Police College in Hendon, England, in 1934. The college was the brainchild of Hugh Trenchard, the Metropolitan Police commissioner. It opened that year and included a forensic lab.

The Locard Exchange Principle states that "Every contact leaves a trace."

A technician puts a blood sample into a centrifuge in a sterile isolated unit.

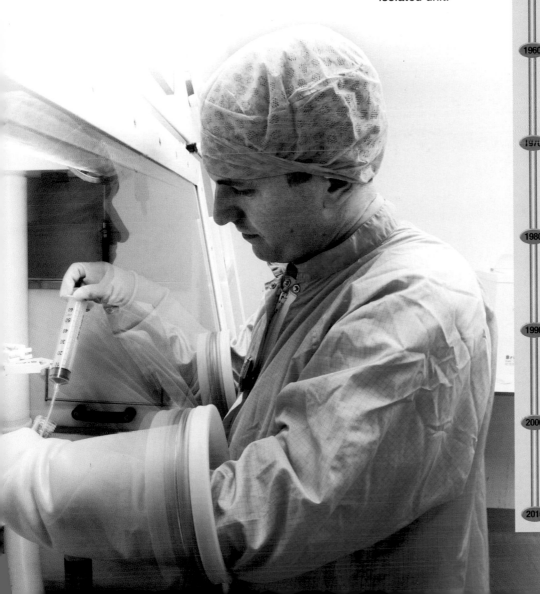

FORENSIC SCIENCE LABORATORY TIMELINE

1920

1930

1910 Edmond Locard opens the world's first forensic laboratory in Lyon, France

1940

1923 The Los Angeles Police Department establishes the U.S.A.'s first forensic lab

1932 The Federal Bureau of Investigation (FBI) in the U.S.A. launches its Technical Laboratory in Washington, D.C.

1950

1935 The Metropolitan Police Laboratory is established at Hendon Police College in London

1960

1936 The Royal Canadian Mounted Police's original forensic laboratory opens in Regina

1970

1957 India establishes its first Central Forensic Laboratory in Calcutta

1975 Ireland's Forensic Science Laboratory opens in Dublin

1980

1991 The United Kingdom's Forensic Science Service is created in London

1990

2005 The South African Police Service establishes its new Criminal Record and Forensic Science Services lab

2000

2006 Pakistan's first forensic laboratory opens in the National Police Bureau in Islamabad

2010

Fingerprints

Fingerprints will always be an uncontested form of identification because no two are alike and a person's prints do not change throughout life.

THE NIGHT STALKER

Richard Ramirez, 25, became known in Los Angeles as "The Night Stalker" when he terrorized the city from June 1984 to August 1985. He sexually attacked and murdered more than a dozen victims, with almost as many surviving other attacks. After the last attack, a teenager wrote down his car's license plate. The vehicle was located and fingerprints taken. The L.A.P.D. had a new AFIS system and matched Ramirez's prints within minutes. Ramirez was convicted and given a life sentence.

The first courts to convict a suspect by fingerprints were in Argentina in 1892 and in England in 1902. Then in 1903, the New York State Prison system began using them for criminal identification. Today fingerprinting remains a major source of identifying criminals, boosted by online databases containing millions of prints of known criminals. Fingerprints are now being scanned electronically into databases, gradually replacing the traditional ink-and-card process. The computerized system, called the Automated Fingerprint Identification System (AFIS), is extremely fast, with computers now able to search through 500,000

FINGERPRINT PATTERNS

The U.K., U.S., and most other English-speaking countries use the Henry System for classifying 10-print collections, developed in 1899 by Sir Edward R. Henry with the British police in India. Three basic types of ridge patterns classify fingerprints:

Arches: these ridges, making up about five percent of all patterns, rise above one another in the centre like an arch. There are plain arches and tented ones that rise more sharply.

Loops: these patterns, about 60 percent of all patterns, are ridges that double back on themselves.

Whorls: these resemble small whirlpools revolving around a point, and make up some 35 percent of patterns. There are four types of whorls.

Arches

Loops

Whorls

prints in less than a second. The system scans prints and plots the positions of ridge characteristics, then compares this with prints in the database. It suggests possible suspects, but the fingerprint expert still makes the final decision. The AFIS is especially valuable in scanning partial prints, using digital enhancement for better contrast and sharpness. It is also able to suggest a match between the broken pattern taken at a crime scene and a complete one on the database.

Australia was the first nation to establish an automatic system. Its National Automated Fingerprint Identification System (NAFIS) began in 1986 and now holds 2.6 million sets of 10-fingerprints. The FBI developed their system in 1991 and today has 47 million such prints, while Britain's system, bearing the same name as Australia's, linked all its forces in 2001 and now has more than five million prints.

In 1986 Australia was the first country to establish an automatic fingerprint ID system.

The identifying characteristics of fingerprints have become standardized.

Trace Evidence

The trace evidence unit of a forensic science lab is the most diverse discipline. Any unknown material that cannot be placed in a specialist unit must go to the trace evidence unit for an attempt to identify it.

THE VALUE OF HAIR

Many cases are solved because hairs have been transferred between a victim and perpetrator. One individual hair can lead to a conviction. Hairs can survive years after a body has decayed, and they hold many secrets within one thin shaft and follicle. They can be a source of DNA, including valuable mitochondrial DNA (mtDNA) passed through maternal generations. Hair also records poisons such as arsenic, and past drug use, including alcohol and nicotine. As well, general racial types can often be determined from samples.

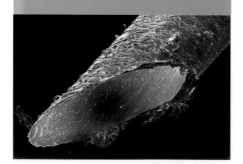

An examiner will investigate a range of items that will include hair, fiber, glass, paint, explosives, footwear and tire impressions, and arson debris. Personal items may include cosmetics such as lipstick, mascara, and nail polish.

The FBI's Trace Evidence Unit maintains reference collections of human and animal hairs, natural and man-made textile fibers, fabrics, feathers, woods, and seeds. Besides testing and matching non-human evidence, the Unit also helps identify

EDMOND LOCARD

The French forensic scientist Edmond Locard (right), the first to declare that "every contact leaves a trace," gave a dramatic description of how trace evidence entraps a criminal:

"Wherever he steps, whatever he touches, whatever he leaves, even unconsciously, will serve as a silent witness against him. Not only his fingerprints or his footprints but his hair, the fibers from his clothes, the glass he breaks, the tool mark he leaves, the paint he scratches, the blood or semen he deposits or collects. All of these, and more, bear mute witness against him. This is evidence that does not forget. It is not confused by the excitement of the moment. It is not absent because human witnesses are. It is factual evidence. Physical evidence cannot be wrong, it cannot perjure itself, it cannot be wholly absent. Only human failure to find it, study, and understand it can diminish its value."

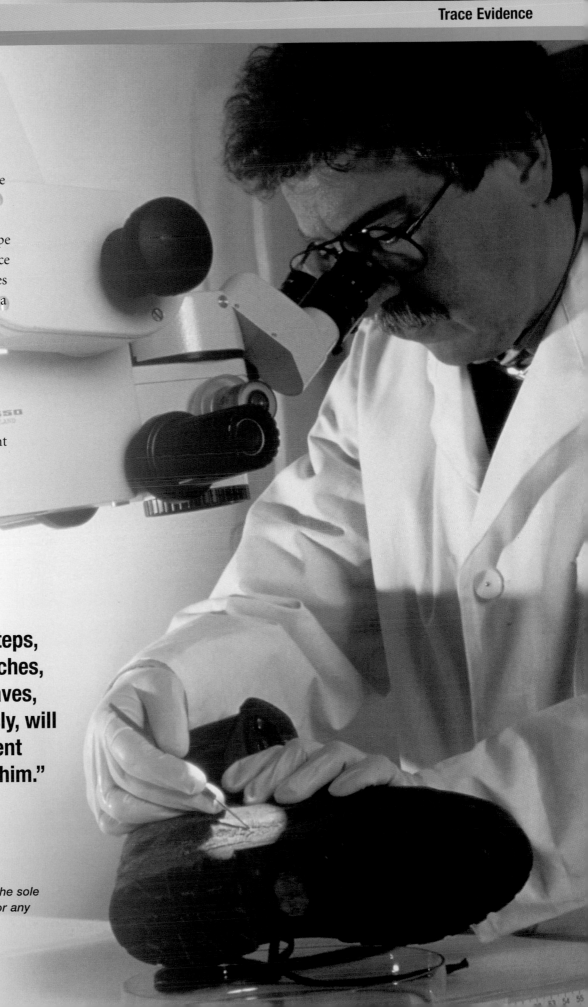

human remains by examining trace samples of teeth and bones.

MICROSCOPES

Various microscopes provide the power to identify and compare trace evidence. A scanning electron microscope (SEM) is used to view surface details that are 100,000 times smaller than the breadth of a hair. Light microscopes can view inside an item of evidence and are normally used to identify hairs. Comparison microscopes have duplicate systems, actually two compound light microscopes, so that two samples can be viewed in a single eyepiece. It is used, for example, to match bullet casings.

"Wherever he steps, whatever he touches, whatever he leaves, even unconsciously, will serve as a silent witness against him."

A forensic expert examines the sole of a shoe searching for soil or any other residue.

What is DNA?

Deoxyribonucleic acid, or DNA, is a six-foot (two-meter) long spiral within every nucleus of our body's cells, which number about 60 trillion. It is located in the nucleus, so it is referred to as nuclear DNA.

It has a double helix structure that looks like a twisted ladder formed into long strands called chromosomes. Inside the spiral are three billion connecting rods that add the "rungs" to the ladder. Known as bases, these are of four different types, which are known as guanine (G), cytosine (C), thymine (T), and adenine (A). The order in which they are positioned along the strand is unique in each person, with the exception of identical twins.

The double helix is formed from pairs of bases, with C only pairing with G and A with T. This never varies, so when DNA replicates itself, all new strands are exact copies. One individual's DNA has six billion bases that create three billion base pairs.

A small section of the DNA spiral contains our genetic code, the genes that give us our looks and characteristics such as curly hair or blue eyes. However, forensic scientists are only interested in the large remainder portion of the spiral. Although it seems to do little and is called "junk" DNA, the short sequences of the base pairs repeat themselves, and this varies greatly among people, allowing individuals to be identified.

Besides nuclear DNA, another type in most cells is mitochondrial DNA (mtDNA), so named for being located in another part of the cell, the mitochondrion. It is arranged in a circle much smaller than the linear nuclear DNA. While nuclear DNA is inherited from each parent equally, mtDNA comes only from the mother, which is vital for tracing direct ancestry.

SIR ALEC JEFFREYS

DNA fingerprinting was discovered and named by the British geneticist Alex Jeffreys on September 10, 1984 in his lab at Leicester University in the UK. He was alone in the darkroom when an X-ray image in the developing tank suddenly gave him the idea that each person has a unique DNA pattern and that this could be used for criminal cases. Born in Oxford in 1950 and graduating from the university there, Jeffreys was knighted in 1994. He remains amazed at his own discovery. "It is the most powerful criminal investigation tool there is," he said. "If you had told me all that 20 years ago, I would not have believed it."

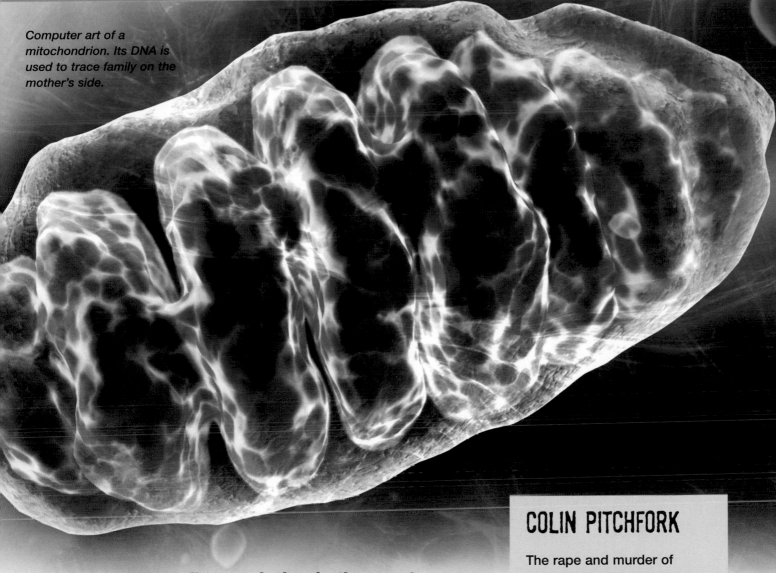

Computer art of a mitochondrion. Its DNA is used to trace family on the mother's side.

"DNA fingerprinting is the most powerful criminal investigation tool there is."

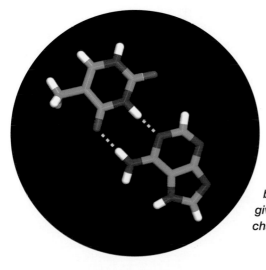

Computer artwork of an A-T (adenine-thymine) base pair. A-T is one of the two base pairs found in DNA (along with C-G (cytosine-guanine)). The positioning of these base pairs along the DNA chain gives organisms their individual characteristics.

COLIN PITCHFORK

The rape and murder of two 15-year-old girls in Narborough, Leicestershire, in England, in 1983 and 1986 led to the world's first forensic application of DNA profiling. Blood samples were taken from the male population of the area, but no match turned up. However, when a woman overheard Ian Kelly boasting he had given a sample for Colin Pitchfork, a local baker, investigators took Pitchfork's sample and it matched. He then confessed and in 1988 was sentenced to life imprisonment.

Taking DNA Samples

The normal method of collecting DNA samples is by swabbing the mouth. The swab is put into the mouth and moved across the inside of the cheek to collect cellular material.

This process of collecting a sample will usually take about 15 minutes. In many countries, trained police officers are supplied with DNA kits that contain everything needed to take a sample, including two swabs and disposable gloves to prevent contamination.

DRAGNET

Mouth swabs are also used in a "sweep" or "dragnet" of people living

A doctor uses a tongue depressor and a swab to take a sample from a girl's throat.

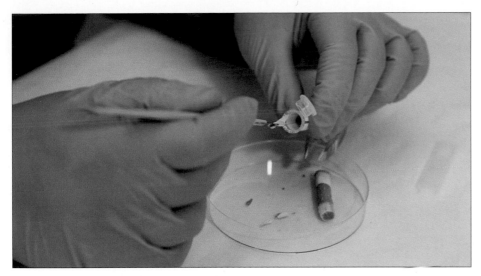

A forensic scientist takes a sample from a cigarette stub to see if traces of DNA from saliva can be found to identify the smoker.

TERESA CORMACK

Patient police in New Zealand tested DNA in a murder case three times in 14 years, certain that advances in the science would eventually lead to the killer. Six-year-old Teresa Cormack was murdered in 1987. DNA swabs were sent to Britain for testing, but they contained insufficient material. More tests in the 1990s were unsuccessful. Then, in 2001, a tiny amount of saved semen was tested with advanced DNA technology. Blood samples were taken from the local male population, and Jules Mikus proved a match. Hairs stored for 14 years were sent to the U.S.A. for mitochondrial DNA testing and confimed the match. Mikus was found guilty in 2002.

in the area of a crime. In the U.S.A., samples from 2,300 men were taken in 1994 in Miami, Florida, when six prostitutes were murdered, and in Baton Rouge, Louisiana, 1,200 men were tested in 2003 during the hunt for a serial killer. The sweeps failed to find the criminals who were arrested by other means, and a 2004 survey at the University of Nebraska at Omaha found that only 1 in 18 sweeps identified the perpetrator.

Mouth swabs for other offences will sometimes lead to an unexpected connection with a previous crime. This happened in 2006 when Sukhdarshan Singh was arrested for drunk driving and police took a mouth swab. His DNA matched the sample taken 18 years before when a woman was raped in Bridgend, Wales. Singh was jailed for four and a half years.

At a crime scene without suspects, common sources of DNA are trace samples of blood, semen, saliva, sweat, hair follicles, bone, and skin. In fact any biological sample with cells is a potential DNA source. Samples are carefully preserved for comparisons with the mouth swabs of suspects and with DNA databases.

BIN LADEN'S DNA

In 2002 the American CBS network reported that the FBI had obtained samples of Osama bin Laden's DNA and were checking it against tissue and body parts on the battlefields of Afghanistan. The sample supposedly was obtained from strands of his hair. One Canadian-led mission that year into the Tora Bora region excavated some 23 graves of al-Qaeda fighters following speculative reports that bin Laden had been killed. DNA samples were taken from the corpses for identification, but the terrorist leader was not among them.

A swab is used to take cells from the inside of the cheek for a DNA sample.

How DNA is Matched

To compare DNA samples an investigator first uses agents such as a chloroform and phenol mixture to separate the DNA from other material in the cell nucleus.

The PCR process will normally amplify this sample. A fluorescent dye is used to tag each DNA fragment.

The double-stranded fragments are converted by chemicals into single strands and separated by length using electrophoresis, in which an electrical current is passed through a sample to move it through a gel or narrow tube, separating the fragments into a series of bands.

VNTRS AND STRS

Forensic investigators check these bands for base sequences that are repeated. The two types are Variable Number Tandem Repeats (VNTRs), which can be hundreds of base pairs long, and Short Tandem Repeats (STRs), which are normally three to seven base pairs long.

PEAK PROFILE

A scanner system reads the sequence: a laser beam causes the dyed fragments to fluoresce, and these flashes are registered on a color-sensitive detector. The results are displayed as colored peaks on a graph. A crime scene DNA will be displayed next to a suspect's sample, and investigators check the results visually or by computer. A match is indicated if the profile of peaks is the same.

A SPEEDIER DNA ANALYSIS

About three hours is required for the replication of DNA by polymerase chain reaction (PCR) to produce a sample large enough to analyze. A new system developed at the University of Michigan, however, will cut the time to 40 minutes.

The DNA mixture must be heated to 203°F/95°C, allowed to cool to 122–140°F/50–60°C, and then heated to 162°F/72°C for the PCR process to work. This must be done 30 to 40 times to get a sufficient sample. The new device uses convection, which keeps the DNA mixture moving in a steady, circular flow within a few minutes. This is done by placing it into a Plexiglas well between two plates held at constant temperatures: 203°F/95°C at the bottom and 122–140°F50–60°C at the top.

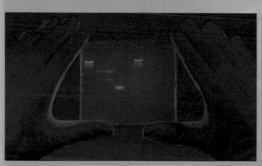

A robot arm picks up a tray of bacterial colonies that clone human DNA fragments for use in the Human Genome Project.

MISINTERPRETING DNA

Forensic experts can draw widely varying conclusions about DNA matches. When Dr. Bradley Schwartz was accused of hiring a hit man to kill his former medical partner, the trial in 2006 turned on disagreements about DNA statistics.

The Department of Public Safety testified that the hit man's DNA matched samples from the crime scene, and only 1 in 20 million people could have such a connection. A DNA expert for the defense reduced those to 1 in 1,658, saying the DNA at the scene had been misinterpreted. But when DNA expert Bruce Budowle of the FBI was called in, he put the number at 1 in 13,000. Dr. Schwartz was convicted and is serving a life sentence.

A researcher uses ultraviolet light to examine an agarose gel containing DNA fragments.

Identifying Crime Victims

Most homicide victims are easily identified, being killed at home or nearby by someone close to them. Other victims are known before they die such as a child who has been abducted.

Yet it is not uncommon for authorities to be baffled by the unknown remains of a victim. The process of identification can take anywhere from days to years, and some bodies are never given a name.

Forensic identity searches rely on several sources, often in combination. They include DNA, dental records, fingerprints, personal effects such as jewelry and clothing, tattoos, birthmarks, scars, as well as the person's age and race. The description is soon given to the news media, normally along with an artist's sketch of the deceased. In skeletal remains, a forensic sculptor may do a facial reconstruction in clay.

REMOVING SIGNS

Visual clues are not always possible. The remains being old, disturbed by animals, or decomposed by the weather can cloud the identification process. Criminals often attempt to remove signs of identification by using fire, quicklime, or acid. In extreme cases, they may mutilate or dismember the body, cutting off the victim's fingers, hands, or even the head.

In rare cases a living victim may be unidentified. Examples involve infants and very young children, victims in a coma or suffering memory loss, and even crime victims who want to remain anonymous.

Vials with DNA samples provided by relatives of the 9/11 victims are stored in the New York City morgue.

WHEN VIEWING FAILS

Matters seem certain when relatives or friends view a body for identification purposes, but this is sometimes unreliable. The body may be burned or disfigured. Or the person identifying can be emotionally upset, too squeamish to take a proper view, or may not have seen the victim for years. In some cases the viewer may give a false identification to cover a crime or gain an inheritance.

Murders have even been committed in order to falsely identify the body. In a U.S. case, Joseph Kalady, facing trial for producing fraudulent documents, killed William White in 2001. Kalady's brother, Michael, falsely identified the body as Kalady's. Investigators, however, identified White through fingerprints, and Kalady was charged with murder, dying in prison in 2003 before the trial.

IDENTIFYING WAR VICTIMS

A team of international forensic experts went to Kosovo for six months in 2002 to identify the remains of victims from the 1999 conflict in which at least 10,000 people are estimated to have been killed or gone missing. The experts included some 80 pathologists, anthropologists, mortuary technicians, liaison officers and information technology experts from Australia, Canada, Costa Rica, Denmark, Italy, Malaysia, Poland, South Africa, Sri Lanka, and the U.S.A.

The examinations were carried out at about 100 burial sites on more than 1250 remains, with the team performing exhumations, autopsies, and identifications before returning the bodies to family members. The project was headed by British Professor Peter Vanezis, director general of the Center for International Forensic Assistance (CIFA), which provides forensic expertise as an instrument for truth and justice.

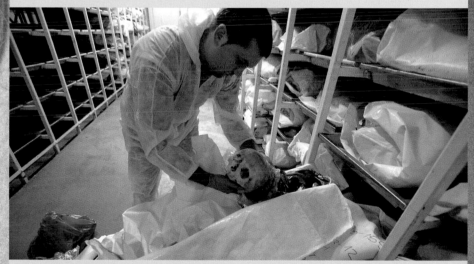

A forensic anthropologist examines remains in Bosnia-Herzegovina for the International Commission on Missing Persons.

In rare cases even a living victim may remain unidentified.

A birthmark such as this 'strawberry' mark can be an invaluable aid in identifying victims.

Fingerprints of Victims

Matching an unknown victim's fingerprints is difficult when the deceased person's prints are not on an official file. However, relatives can bring personal objects which might bear the victim's prints.

D ifficulties often exist in fingerprinting the dead because of deterioration of the skin. Testifying in 2004 at a court case concerning a 1976 murder, retired FBI agent John Munis said the body had decomposed, causing the hands to shrivel and the fingers to close. A pathologist had to remove the hands and they were shipped in individual containers to the FBI laboratory that secured prints and identification.

Technology now allows identity searches to be done from a crime scene. The Garda, Ireland's police, has a new Fingerprint Mobile Laboratory Vehicle to allow the scanning of prints at the scene. These are sent back by telephone lines to the Technical Bureau for instant processing.

While massive databases exist of criminal fingerprints, other sources must be explored to identify ordinary victims. Fingerprints, for instance, are taken and filed by the military and some employers; they also exist on biometric cards used for security access. Non-criminal databases are rapidly increasing for security reasons. The U.S.A. already tracks foreign visitors by using electronically scanned fingerprints, and all new European passports will include two fingerprints from early 2008.

The U.S.A. already tracks foreign visitors by using electronically scanned fingerprints.

THE BLACK DAHLIA

One of Hollywood's most gruesome murders came to light on January 15, 1947 when the body of a nude young woman was discovered in Los Angeles. She had been cut in half and undergone other mutilations. Detectives had no idea who she was. They took fingerprints and gave them to the Los Angeles Examiner, which enlarged and sent them to the FBI in Washington, D.C. Their database then had 104 million prints on file, mostly criminals. This time they were lucky, matching them to Elizabeth Short, 22, who had been fingerprinted twice: for a job at a California army base, and for her arrest for underage drinking. Friends had nicknamed her "Black Dahlia" for doing her black hair in a flowerlike style and for wearing black garments.

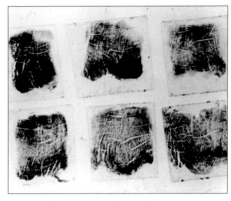

These fingerprints from the corpse of the "Black Dahlia" identified her as Elizabeth Short.

LIVESCAN FOR THE DEAD

In 2006 the University of Leicester in England, working with the Leicester Constabulary and the Institute of Legal Medicine at the University of Hamburg, demonstrated the first use of an electronic hand-held device to recover fingerprints from the dead. It was developed from the larger Livescan computer device that takes prints from fingers pressed against a coated glass platform.

The UK Home Office introduced Livescan itself to all police forces in 2007. The state of California has not accepted inked fingerprint cards since 2005, only Livescan images.

A US official checks fingerprints of a tourist crossing from Canada to Niagara Falls, New York.

Dental Identification

Dental records are extremely valuable in establishing an unknown identity. Teeth are especially hard and almost indestructible, remaining after burial in earth and water for years and even surviving fire.

The impressions of each individual's teeth are different, due to chips, fillings, misalignments and missing teeth.

Dentists routinely make notes about the surfaces of each patient's 32 adult teeth.

A comparison with dental records,

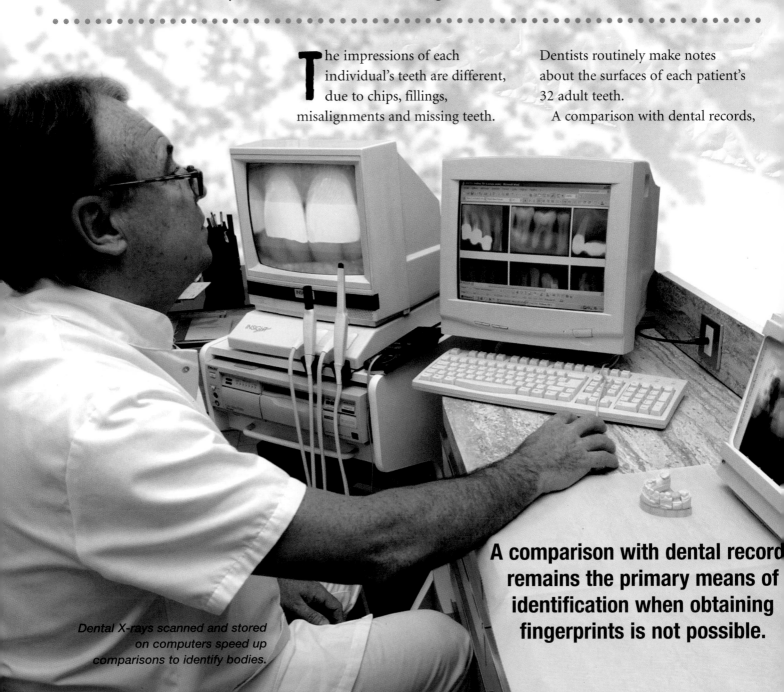

Dental X-rays scanned and stored on computers speed up comparisons to identify bodies.

A comparison with dental record remains the primary means of identification when obtaining fingerprints is not possible.

which most people have, still remains the primary means of identification when obtaining fingerprints is not possible. DNA technology, in contrast, is expensive and often obtaining results takes weeks or months. Dental records are also much cheaper to enter onto a database.

In identifying crime victims, a total and accurate dental examination should be made, including X-rays of the teeth and jaws, which can now be done with a portable instrument at the crime scene. Forensic odontologists can compare several areas with dental records, including the number of teeth, cavities and fillings, bridges, restoration, spacing, and special details such as an overbite or overlap of teeth. As well, the materials and methods used in dental work can indicate the country where the treatment was administered.

DENTAL IDENTIFICATIONS IN HISTORY

The unique marks of teeth have been used throughout history: The Roman emperor Nero identified his mother Agrippina, whom he had murdered in 59 C.E., by her teeth. William the Conqueror used to bite the wax seals on his letters with his crooked teeth to verify they were from him. The first formally reported case of dental identification was for John Talbot, the Earl of Shrewsbury, who fell at the battle of Castillon in France in 1453.

Sir John Talbot died on 17 July 1453 at the battle of Castillon during the Hundred Years War.

The American patriot Paul Revere was able to identify his friend Dr. Joseph Warren 10 months after he was buried, a victim of the 1775 Battle of Bunker Hill in Massachusetts. This was an easy identification, because Revere had fashioned dentures for Warren. In 1865 a dental identification was made of John Wilkes Booth, the assassin of President Abraham Lincoln.

The first disaster victims to be identified by their teeth were killed in a fire in 1849 at the Vienna Opera House. Dental records were also used to establish identity after 126 rich Parisians who were killed in 1897 in a charity bazaar fire.

PROBLEMS OF DENTAL IDENTIFICATIONS

Despite the hardiness of teeth and the prevalence of dental records, problems may be encountered with this type of identification. In some cases, investigators encounter partial or no dental records, or may fail to recover all teeth and their restorations. Even the improvement of dental health, thanks to the use increasing of fluoridation, works against identification because it means people generally have fewer cavities and restorations. In addition laws also exist in some countries, such as the U.S.A., to protect medical records and therefore may slow an investigation slightly.

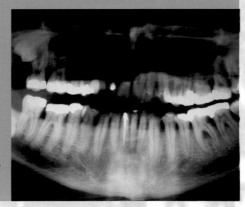
Dental fillings help identifications. The white areas in the teeth of this 45-year-old man show teeth with fillings.

49

Skin Marks

Some of the most distinctive marks of identification are found on the skin. Birthmarks, scars, and tattoos are easy to recognize, such as the red birthmark on the forehead of the former Russian president Mikhail Gorbachev.

Such marks have been important indicators throughout history. King Harold's body was identified after the battle of Hastings by a tattoo over his heart, reading "Edith and England."

TATTOOS

Tattoos, in fact, have now become acceptable body decorations, including those worn by celebrities such as international sports and film stars. Their permanence and their prevalence among criminals has proved to be a blessing to police. Especially helpful are the chosen names or slogans, as used by gang members. When identifying corpses, investigators try to match the tattoos to the known work of tattoo artists. Sometimes pigments from the skin are even extracted and analyzed to trace the source. Another recent trend, piercing the ears, nose, eyebrows and other body parts, is also a strong indicator for identification.

"SCARFACE"

Forensic investigators also look for scars acquired from operations, plastic surgery, or fights. The gangster Al Capone was nicknamed "Scarface" after his cheek was cut with a knife during a dispute in his early days. Birthmarks have fine identifying characteristics because they have irregular shapes, and skin blemishes such as moles have been used to identify bodies.

NATASCHA KAMPUSCH

A pale and distressed 18-year-old girl ran to an elderly man on August 23, 2006 in Vienna, Austria, saying she had escaped after being kidnapped and held captive. Her name, she said, was Natascha Kampusch. This was verified by her family who identified her by a scar on her upper arm that went back to an operation she had as a child. The identity resolved one of Austria's best-known criminal mysteries. Hours after her escape, the man who had snatched her from a Vienna street and held her for eight years, committed suicide by throwing himself in front of a train.

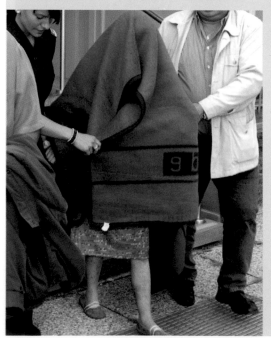

Covered by a blanket, Natascha Kampusch is escorted by police on the day she escaped.

King Harold's body was identified after the battle of Hastings by a tattoo over his heart, reading "Edith and England."

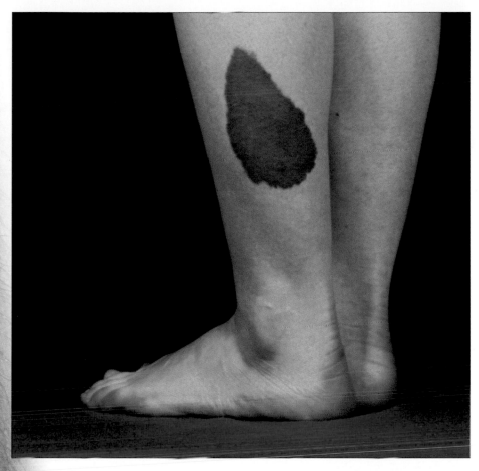

Birthmarks have led to numerous identifications such as this large pigmented one on a young woman's calf. These will occur in different forms, with some composed of small blood vessels, including the strawberry mark, and some being like a port-wine stain.

Scars such as this one on the forearm of a male patient are excellent identification marks.

THE SHARK ARM CASE

A tiger shark caught by fishermen was an attraction in Coogee, Australia, on April 25, 1935 at the nation's annual Anzac Day celebration. Fun became fear, however, when the animal suddenly thrashed about and coughed up a tattooed human arm. Searches for the rest of the body all failed. The fingerprints were found to be those of James Smith, a construction worker, and his wife identified his arm from the tattoo showing two sparring boxers.

After this identification, the renowned English forensic pathologist Sir Sydney Smith examined the arm and said it had been cut off rather than bitten off by the shark. This indicated murder, because Smith had been involved in the drugs trade. A key witness was subsequently murdered, and an inquest was abandoned due to an old law that said a body was necessary and "a limb does not constitute a body."

Facial Reconstruction

When only a skull is recovered from a nameless crime victim, forensic sculptors may be called in to reconstruct the face in modeling clay, a highly skilled procedure.

The likeness of a living person is difficult to recreate, but the skull gives an indication of the form and contours needed. The "American model," devised in the U.S.A., uses knowledge of the tissue depth that covers the various bony landmarks of a skull. There are from 20 to 35 tissue depths to contend with around the face, and the forensic artist has known measurements for different ages, sexes, and ethnic groups.

The process begins with small wooden depth pegs, often toothpicks, fixed to the skull or a cast at the different tissue depths. Strips of clay "muscles" are applied, with their thickness measured to the height of the pegs. The sculptor then fills the gaps between the strips, smoothes out the clay, removes the pegs, and begins modeling the nose (the most difficult because of the lack of bone), eyes, mouth, ears, chin, and jowls. Prosthetic eyeballs are placed into the eye sockets to increase the realistic look.

The artist must make several guesses, including the plumpness of the face, hairstyle, structure of the eyelids, and facial expressions. As well, the recovered skull is often just a portion whose shape must be filled in.

A forensic sculptor carefully works on a model of a dead person's head. Such models can be used to construct a likeness of a person from their remains, aiding in the identification process.

COMPUTER FACIAL RECONSTRUCTION

Digital reconstruction is the latest tool in identifying crime victims. A scan is taken of the skull as it rotates on a turntable, and the computer program creates a digital skull that can be manipulated on the screen. The technician then selects a computer tomography (CT) three-dimensional scan of a real person estimated to be the same race and about the same age. As this scan is digitally merged with the one of the skull, it adjusts to correspond and moves its facial tissue into a shape that resembles the victim. The hair and eyes are estimated and added to provide a lifelike image. Computer reconstruction has the value of giving a view from any angle, but retains the limitations of clay reconstruction.

The Unit of Forensic Art, opened in 2005 at the University of Dundee, has a groundbreaking program that allows the user to "feel" the surface of the reconstructed face on the screen.

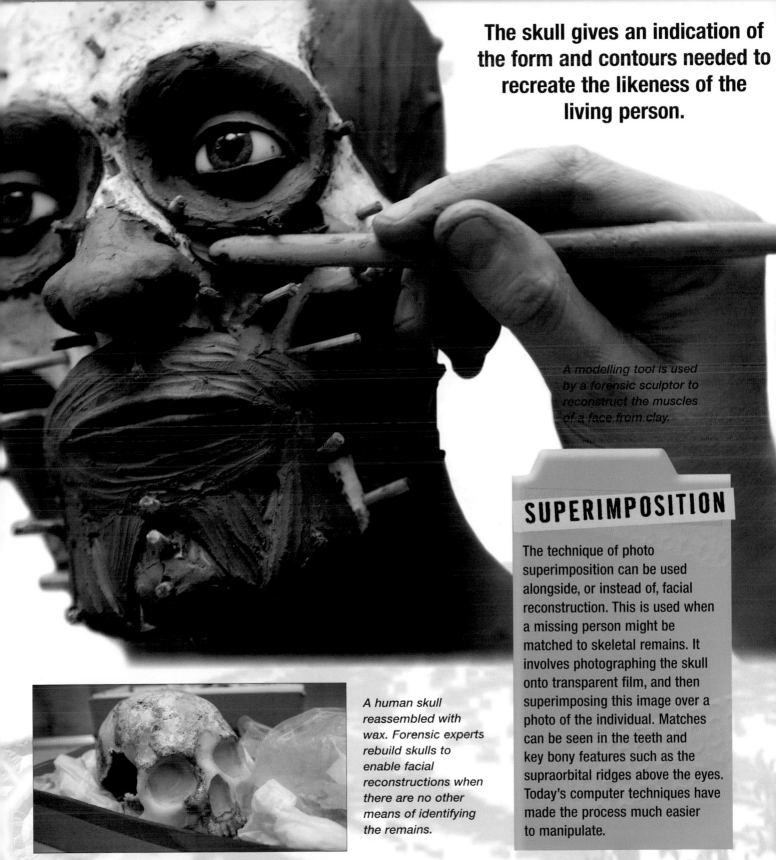

The skull gives an indication of the form and contours needed to recreate the likeness of the living person.

A modelling tool is used by a forensic sculptor to reconstruct the muscles of a face from clay.

A human skull reassembled with wax. Forensic experts rebuild skulls to enable facial reconstructions when there are no other means of identifying the remains.

SUPERIMPOSITION

The technique of photo superimposition can be used alongside, or instead of, facial reconstruction. This is used when a missing person might be matched to skeletal remains. It involves photographing the skull onto transparent film, and then superimposing this image over a photo of the individual. Matches can be seen in the teeth and key bony features such as the supraorbital ridges above the eyes. Today's computer techniques have made the process much easier to manipulate.

53

The Forensic Pathologist

The forensic pathologist can be the most important scientist in an investigation because he or she knows several medical disciplines and will most likely be involved throughout a case.

This can begin at the crime scene, where the pathologist may be able to give an opinion on both the cause and manner of death after viewing the evidence *in situ*.

MYSTERY POISONING

Such was the case when two British children were found dead in 2006 in a Corfu hotel bungalow alongside their comatose father and his partner. Dr. Stephanos Gasteratos, the Corfu hospital pathologist, said this was most likely a case of a strong poison, but not food poisoning. There were no signs of forced entry, struggle, or other clues. Toxicology tests revealed they had died of carbon monoxide poisoning, traced to an overheated boiler.

As the investigation moves to the lab, a forensic pathologist will consult with other specialists such as a forensic toxicologist if poison is suspected or a forensic odontologist for identification. Forensic pathologists also perform autopsies to gather evidence about sudden and apparently unexplained deaths. They write up the results and submit a report, along with photographs and documents, to the coroner. Their findings are explained in terms of the police investigation so the report will serve as proper evidence in court.

Forensic pathologists work to identify mudslide victims in the Philippines in 2006. Fingertips were removed for fingerprints.

TOOLS OF THE PATHOLOGIST

A pathologist works in three main areas and requires different tools and equipment for each:

Crime scene—The initial investigation on site requires a kit containing items such as a fingerprint brush, aluminum dusting powder, lifting tape, magnifying glass, cotton swabs, and small sample containers. The pathologist will also need protective clothing and work with police equipment such as body bags.

Laboratory—A pathologist usually heads a crime laboratory and has access to all available equipment, from electron microscopes to test tubes and complex analysis instruments. Much of this work involves collaboration with colleagues in their areas of specialization.

Autopsy room—Here the pathologist is on the familiar ground of a surgeon aided by assistants. Because the morgue is an operating room for the dead, the tools consist of items such as a scalpel, bone cutters, cranium chisel, handsaw, and brain knife.

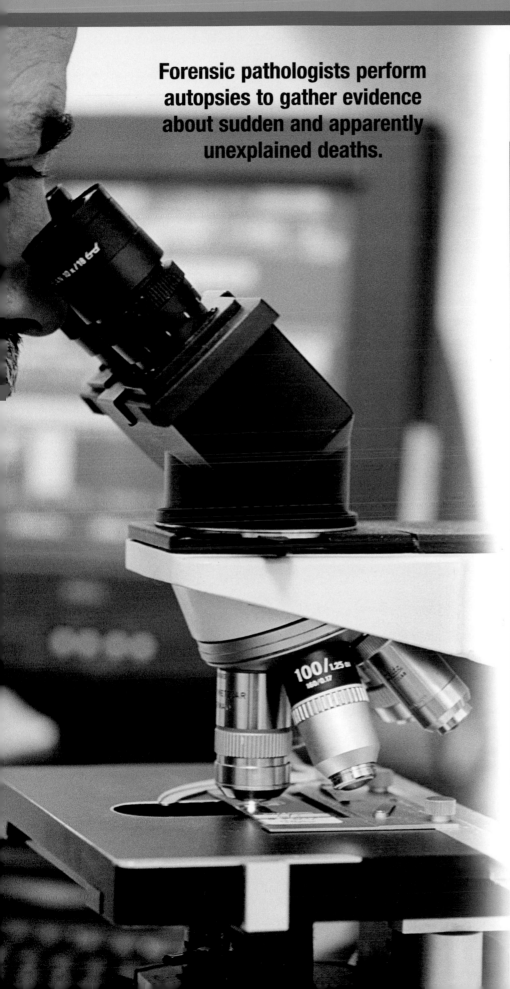

Forensic pathologists perform autopsies to gather evidence about sudden and apparently unexplained deaths.

THE REAL SHERLOCK HOLMES

When Arthur Conan Doyle was a medical student at the University of Edinburgh in 1877, he was impressed by one of his professors, Dr. Joseph Bell (above), who was a pioneering forensic pathologist. Doyle became his assistant and was able to absorb his tutor's keen eye for details. Bell would often observe the walk and accent of strangers and identify where they came from and their professions.

Later, when Doyle created his fictional sleuth, Sherlock Holmes, he loosely based him on Bell, who supposedly would say, "It was elementary," when diagnosing a patient.

A forensic pathologist seeks a conclusive result by analyzing a sample under a microscope.

The Autopsy

An autopsy is used to establish the cause of death. It will involve more than the opening of the body. A photographer will also be present to photograph the body laid out in the morgue.

A photographer will be present to photograph the body laid out in the morgue. The first photos will record the corpse in the clothing worn when found, and each time the pathologist removes a piece, another photo will be taken.

Before the dissection, the pathologist will measure and weigh the body and record the age, sex, race, and hair and eye colors. Then the pathologist will check the clothes for trace evidence, check for marks on the skin, collect a sample of hair, and clip or scrape the fingernails. Swabs will be taken from the mouth, rectum, and sexual organs. X-rays may also be taken, because these will reveal the size and shape of knife wounds and how, for example, bullets moved through the body.

Dissecting the body normally follows a set routine. An incision is made, organs such as the heart and lungs removed and weighed, the abdomen examined, and samples taken from the stomach. The skull is then opened to view the brain. Finally the organs are returned to the body, which is closed with sutures and released to the family for burial.

AUTOPSY N
WT.
BRAIN
LIVER
SPLEEN
PANCREAS
THYROID
ADRENALS
UTERUS
TESTES
THYMUS
KIDNEYS
LUNGS
HEART

CHRIS PENN

When the actor Chris Penn died unexpectedly in Santa Monica, California, on January 24, 2006, an immediate postmortem examination was unable to determine how he died. There were no obvious signs of foul play or suicide. However, the 40-year-old younger brother of actor Sean Penn had a history of drug abuse.

A Los Angeles coroner ordered a blood toxicology test. When this was added to the earlier autopsy, it was found that Penn had died of an enlarged heart and the effects of mixing several medications.

Chris Penn died the day before his film, "The Darwin Awards", premiered at the Sundance Film Festival.

This autopsy room in a hospital morgue has scales used to weigh the major organs.

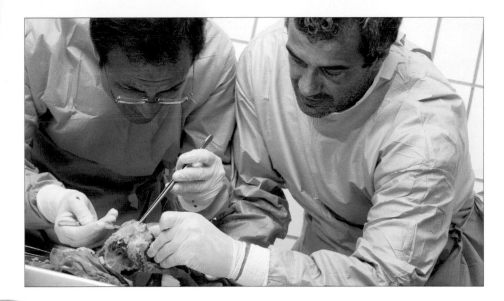

These forensic pathologists wear latex gloves to dissect the shoulder of a cadaver during an autopsy. Others present at the examination may include a police witness and an exhibits officer who examines materials on the body.

Before the dissection, the pathologist will measure and weigh the body.

A MUSLIM AUTOPSY

Although Islam requires that a dead body be buried quickly without cutting or disturbing it, the Maldives' government approved that Muslim country's first autopsy in April 2007 after a request by the relatives of the deceased. This followed the death of Hussain Salah, a Maldivian opposition activist. His Maldivian Democratic Party accused prison authorities of beating him to death. A government spokesman said Salah had been released from prison from a narcotics charge, and his body was found floating in the sea. The government flew Salah's body to Sri Lanka for the autopsy. Dr LBL De Alwis, the chief judicial medical officer of Sri Lanka, conducted the postmortem examination and found that Salah drowned. He said minor injuries to the nose, face and left leg could have been sustained in the water. "There were no major injuries to bones, soft tissue, or internal organs," he said, "and therefore death by physical violence is excluded."

Dissecting the Body

A dissection begins with an incision down the front of a cadaver, but the manner of the cutting will depend upon whether the death seems natural or suspicious.

• •

If natural, one simple incision is made from the larynx to the pubic region and the organs removed for examination. If the deceased is a possible victim of crime, a cut in the shape of a T or Y is done to provide better access to the body cavity.

The ribs and clavicles are cut and the breastplate removed. Samples are taken of fluids such as blood, bile, and urine for analysis. All of these could reveal any drugs taken hours before the death.

A pathologist may remove the major organs together such as the heart, lungs, trachea, and esophagus, but they are sometimes removed

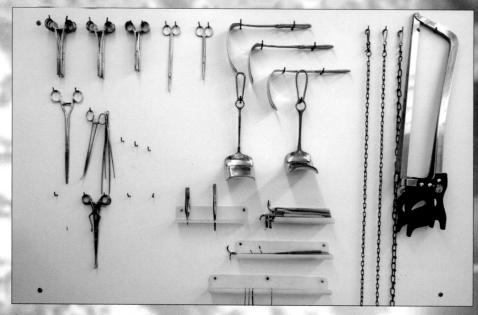

Autopsy instruments include the bone cutter and cranium chisel.

separately. The organs are weighed, and samples taken for microscopic examination. The contents of the stomach and intestine are inspected and samples also taken for toxicological tests.

Cutting the scalp and then sawing open the skull reveals the brain. The pathologist views the brain in place and then removes it for a closer examination. Thin slices of the brain tissue are taken for a microscopic exam.

Although the torso is normally dissected first, if there is evidence of the victim having been strangled, the pathologist will begin the autopsy with the head and neck.

TWO TYPES OF AUTOPSIES

If a death is presumed to be unknown or suspicious, a legal authority asks for a medico-legal autopsy, sometimes called a forensic autopsy. The unknown death will often have no foul play suspected. This type of autopsy is only carried out in the U.S.A. by certified forensic pathologists, or in some cases by hospital pathologists who are designated medical examiners.

A clinical autopsy, also known as an academic or hospital autopsy, is performed to verify a cause of death that is usually known such as cancer or a stroke. They are also used to judge the effectiveness of treatment, study the processes of a disease and educate medical students and personnel. These autopsies cannot be performed without the consent of the next of kin of the deceased.

The hand of a woman is shown here during an autopsy. She had been dead for two days.

If the deceased is a possible victim of crime, a cut in the shape of a T or Y is made to provide better access to the body cavity.

THE FIRST AUTOPSIES

Around 300 B.C.E., the Greek anatomist Herophilus was conducting dissections to teach human anatomy, and a century later the Greek physician Erasistratus of Ceos began using them in order to understand diseases. In the late 1400s the Italian physician Antonio Benivieni published the first book concerning anatomical pathology, *Remarkable Hidden Causes of Disease*. In the eighteenth century, the French physician Marie François Xavier Bichat conducted more than 600 autopsies.

Sir William Osler, a Canadian physician, was a great promoter of the autopsy in the late nineteenth century. He wrote that investigating the causes of death in this manner to prevent and treat disease "is one of the highest objects of the physician."

The French pathologist Marie-François Xavier Bichat (1771–1802) worked in a Paris hospital for the poor and founded modern histology, the study of tissues.

59

Trace Evidence

Although trace evidence is more associated with identifying a suspect, it is also of value in finding the cause of death. Both mysteries can be solved at the same time.

For example a trace of arsenic in soup will confirm the cause of a victim's death and immediately point to the spouse as the prime suspect. Other cases have identified the cause but not the criminal. When the former Russian spy Alexander Litvinenko died in London in 2006, pathologists found traces of polonium 210, a lethal radioactive substance, but police could only theorize over a Russian connection.

Traces of drugs near bodies are strong indicators of an overdose.

Autopsies also turn up traces within a body that will overturn the original conjecture of death. This occurred in a Florida case in 2005. In Wellington, a husband and father, aged in his late forties, died in his sleep apparently of a heart attack. An autopsy, however, found he had overdosed on a combination of cocaine and oxycodone.

Homicides can also be revealed by drug traces in the body. In 2006 Daniela Toledo do Prado brought her convulsive daughter, Vittoria, to a hospital in Sâo Paulo, Brazil, saying she had drunk spoiled milk. After the child died of heart failure the next day, doctors found a suspicious white powder on the girl's tongue. The mother said it was milk, but tests identified it as cocaine. Traces were later found in the baby's bottle, and the mother was charged with murder.

MARILYN MONROE'S AUTOPSY

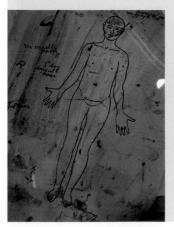

Marilyn Monroe died on August 4,1962, and her autopsy was conducted by Dr Thomas Noguchi. Afterward, Coroner Theodore Curphey said she died from an overdose of barbiturates. Traces of the drug pentobarbital (sleeping pills) were discovered in her liver and chloral hydrate in her blood. He ruled her death a "probable suicide." Despite this many still believe it was accidental and conspiracy theorists say it was murder.
The autopsy consisted of a Y-shaped incision. A sample of blood was taken, and the liver, kidney, stomach and contents, urine, and intestine were saved for further toxicological study. Her brain was weighed at 50.79 oz/1440 g and her heart at 10.58 oz/300 g.

This sketch was part of the Coroner's Autopsy Report on Marilyn Monroe's death. The report was featured in an exhibit about the star in the Hollywood Museum.

Craig Harvey, chief at the Los Angeles County Coroners Office, handles a body in the crypt. Some are stored for up to seven years.

HOW HAIR TRAVELS

Forensic research carried out in Australia reveals that hair found at a crime scene may not indicate a suspect, since it could have been transferred several times. Josephine Dachs investigated how hair clings to different fabrics while she worked in forensic services at the Australian Federal Police. The results were published in the journal *Forensic Science International*.

Dachs found that hair is easily passed on in a car, by contacting someone else or even through washing clothes. For her research she attached stray hairs to people who then went about their normal activities. A lot was lost in the first hour or so through movement, but several stayed put for some time.

Los Angeles County Coroner Dr Lakshmanan Sathyavagiswaran presents evidence during the 1995 O. J. Simpson murder trial.

61

The Forensic Artist

In the world of modern technology, the sketchpad is not dead. Photofit composites and E-FIT computer programs are now available to create a criminal's facial features.

After the 1995 bombing of the U.S. Federal Building in Oklahoma City, which killed 168 people, an FBI forensic artist, Raymond Rozycki, met for two to three hours with a witness.

To create an accurate sketch Rozycki showed the witness the FBI's facial catalog. It contains photographs of faces broken down by the overall shape and separate characteristics such as eyes, eyebrows, cheeks, chin, ear, and hair. Each of the 25 categories has 16 different photographs. After the parts were selected and combined, Rozycki used further details from the witness to fine-tune the drawing. The witness described the man who rented the van that carried the bomb. The resulting sketch Rozycki made identified the bomber as Timothy McVeigh, and he was soon apprehended.

CCTV EVIDENCE

Artists are also asked to make sketches from surveillance-camera evidence in order to clarify and simplify the images. This happened after a suicide car bombing on

March 2, 2006, near the American consulate in Karachi, Pakistan, which killed one diplomat and four other people. A day later, the Pakistani police artist drew a sketch from camera images and eyewitness accounts.

The sketch by FBI forensic artist Raymond Rozycki produced a striking resemblance to the bomber Timothy McVeigh.

Timothy McVeigh is escorted in 1995 by authorities to the courthouse in Oklahoma City.

ARTISTIC AGING

Forensic artists also help find people who have been missing for several years. This is done by "age progression." The artist uses photographs and knowledge of the growth of bone structure to create a sketch of how the person might have aged, as seen in this computer imaging of Elvis Presley. Such artists work, for instance, for the U.K.'s National Missing Persons Helpline.

One manner of estimating advanced age involves siblings. If the missing person has a brother or sister, the artist can use a photograph of the sibling and merge it with an old photo of the missing person. A computer program will show how the face might have matured.

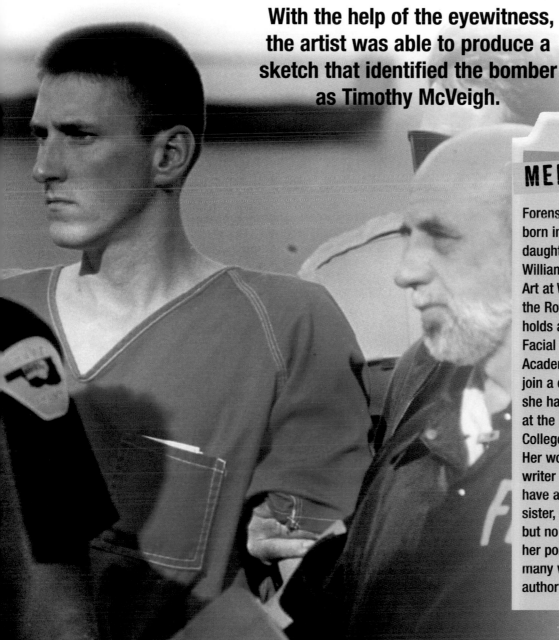

With the help of the eyewitness, the artist was able to produce a sketch that identified the bomber as Timothy McVeigh.

MELISSA DRING

Forensic artist Melissa Dring was born in Winchester, England, the daughter of the portrait painter William Dring, RA. She studied Fine Art at Winchester School of Art and the Royal Academy Schools, and holds a degree in the Psychology of Facial Identification. The FBI Police Academy in Virginia invited her to join a course for police artists, and she has since taught such courses at the Durham Police Training College.

Her work includes a portrait of the writer Jane Austen as she might have appeared as an adult. Her sister, Cassandra, sketched Austen but no definitive portrait exists. For her portrait Dring was helped by the many written accounts of the author's looks.

E-FIT Programs

The reconstruction of a suspect's face was done by identikit and from 1970 mostly by photofit. Both require a witness to select a series of different facial features and fit them together like a jigsaw puzzle.

Identikit uses sketches, and photofit uses photographs. With the advent of computers, the old system, which produced rather disjoined images, was replaced by the electronic facial identification technique, commonly known as E-FIT, a name coined by Janina Kaminska at the U.K. Home Office in 1984.

An E-FIT software program, which stores hundreds of facial features, is used by such law enforcement agencies as Scotland Yard, the FBI, and the Royal Canadian Mounted Police. This computerized photofit system is also a feature of the BBC's Crimewatch television program.

In 2005 advanced E-FITs were unveiled in London at a conference on crime-fighting technology. The software now uses a genetic algorithm to mutate a screen image as the witness gives the description. This cuts down the old selection of parts from hours to minutes.

One system, EigenFit, has been developed at the University of Kent, in England, and another, EvoFit, at the University of Stirling, in Scotland. Both packages produce nine random faces based on the sex, race, and hairstyle of the suspect. The witness chooses the closest likeness, and then the program evolves the face according to additional details given. A more realistic face is created by the program's attention to variations in a face's shape, shading, and the relationship between the features.

Detective Chief Inspector Stuart Mace talks with the press after releasing E-FIT images of the suspect who shot a 19-year-old woman in Walthamstow, London on New Year's Day 2002 to steal her cellphone. The victim was left with a gash on her forehead and recovered.

STUYVESANT TOWN RAPIST

Detective Stephen Mancusi, the senior forensic artist with the New York Police Department, has had many successes. However the most unusual one involved the "Stuyvesant Town Rapist," who had raped four women in that residential area of Manhattan.

The last victim recalled the rapist's features and worked with Mancusi on a composite sketch. It was quickly printed on posters and distributed around the city. A Bronx assistant district attorney spotted one and immediately recognized her half-brother, Anthony Mane. He was arrested, convicted, and sentenced to up to 40 years.

Above: A crime victim (left) works with a police artist to create a computerized image of the criminal.

A man's head is overlaid with a contour map to produce a computerized facial image. The grid compares specific points.

TERESA REDMON

When Teresa Redmon began working as a forensic artist for the Kentucky State Police in 1994, she created her composite sketches of criminals and missing persons by drawing them by hand. More recently, the police have invested in software technology, and Redmon chose E-FiT because it was the one that focused solely on law enforcement and, she notes, contained the world's largest database of hairstyles, facial features and other attributes. From the first 14 E-FIT composite faces she created, the police made ten arrests, and the overall successful rate now is 80 percent. Today, as she travels in Kentucky working with state and local police, she carries along her laptop computer loaded with E-FIT and other face composite systems.

Surveillance Cameras

They may give fuzzy, jerky images, but closed-circuit television (CCTV) cameras have proved invaluable in identifying criminals and tracing the last movements of victims.

Closed-circuit television (CCTV) cameras, such as the one pictured left, beam their images back to monitors in a security control room.

SWISS VANDAL

Surveillance cameras in Thailand caught a drunk Swiss man spraying black paint on several portraits of the Thai king Bhumibol Adulyadej and this led in March 2007 to a sentence of ten years in prison. Oliver Jufer, 57, at first blamed a German who had left for the Philippines, but decided to confess after the cameras recorded his vandalism. He could have received 75 years, but the judge reduced the sentence because he had confessed. Jufer has lived in Thailand for a decade, and the 79-year-old monarch had studied in Switzerland. The king had previously said he would pardon anyone jailed for insulting him.

Technical advances now allow the captured faces of suspects to be compared with mug shots by using imaginary points, or "landmarks," on the faces.

Cameras have also been successful in locating vulnerable missing persons and for preventive surveillance such as locating soccer hooligans in a crowd.

WATCHING THE POLICE

There are an estimated 25 million CCTV cameras in the world. In 2007 Britain led all countries in having up to 4.2 million, with a city person's image captured about 300 times a day. Some worry this is an invasion of privacy, but the Association of Chief Police Officers (ACPO) said many safeguards are in place to stop abuses by officers. "The police use of surveillance," said ACPO's Graham Gerrard, "is probably the most regulated of any group in society."

In some areas of Britain, CCTV has reduced crime by 95 percent. In the Wakefield District of West Yorkshire during the first quarter of 2006, a total of 401 arrests were due to the 68 cameras in the center of the city of Wakefield and a further 80 across the district.

SURVEILLANCE SLIPS

The value of CCTV is especially appreciated when cameras fail.

This occurred during the London bombings of July 7, 2005, when the camera was not working on the bus that was attacked. Police have stressed that tapes must be changed daily and tested, and that the time and date displays need to be correct.

A CCTV camera observes passengers on a London bus. These cameras, used as deterrents and for evidence of crimes, will be on all London buses in 2007.

SHOPLIFTING

Private surveillance cameras are making it much easier to catch shoplifters. One of the famous catches was American actress Winona Ryder, who was filmed in 2001 in the Beverly Hills Saks Fifth Avenue store as she stole more than 20 items worth $5560. A Saks security guard, who operated the cameras from a basement control room, played the videotape during Ryder's trial in 2002. It showed her entering a dressing room in the store's luxury boutique carrying a red bag, then leaving with the bag looking much larger. She also bought items during her hour-and-a-half visit. The cameras helped convict Ryder, who was given a three-year probation, 480 hours of community service, $2700 in fines and ordered to pay Saks for the stolen items.

Identification by Witnesses

Witnesses can be unsure and unreliable, but they are the key to countless arrests and convictions.

Witnesses provide the descriptions used by forensic artists, they recognize faces displayed on posters and television crime programs, they attend line-ups to point out the perpetrator, and they provide anonymous tips.

Problems do exist because anyone's memory may play tricks. Some witnesses, as well, may have reasons to make incorrect identifications. For these reasons, a great effort is made to back up witness statements with physical forensic evidence. In 1994 in the U.S.A., a 13-year-old girl identified Peter Rose of Lodi, California, as the person who had dragged her into an alley and raped her. In 2004 the girl admitted she had no idea who had attacked her and, after serving ten years in jail, Rose was proven innocent by DNA tests.

Testimony can endanger the life of a witness, and some have been murdered. Several U.K. police forces run dedicated witness support schemes, while the U.S.A. and Canada have legislated formal protection programs. Since it began in 1970, the U.S. Federal Witness Security Program has given protection, relocation and new identities to more than 7,500 witnesses and 9,500 witness family members.

This pilot, being sworn in before giving evidence against Panamanian General Noriega in 1988, is wearing a hood to protect his identity.

"I WAS CERTAIN, BUT I WAS WRONG"

Writing in the *New York Times*, Jennifer Thompson described how convinced she was in making an identification after being raped in 1984. She had studied every detail on her attacker's face, and later confidently identified him from police photos, in a line-up, and again during the trial in 1986. Because of this, Ronald Cotton was given a life sentence.

When another man, named Bobby Poole, bragged about the rape, police brought him to Jennifer who said she had never seen him before in her life. Eleven years after Cotton's conviction, in 1995, Jennifer gave blood so DNA tests could finally resolve the doubts. They proved she had identified the wrong man. Poole was the rapist, and he confessed. "I live with constant anguish that my profound mistake cost him so dearly," she said after Cotton's release.

Some witnesses may have reasons to make incorrect identifications.

"IVAN THE TERRIBLE"

When John Demjanjuk was accused of being "Ivan the Terrible," a notorious SS guard at the Treblinka concentration camp during World War II, the U.S. extradited him to Israel in 1986. During his trial there, despite the passage of nearly 50 years, five witnesses identified him in court and six others also did from photographs. Even a former SS guard agreed.

In 1988, the court in Jerusalem sentenced him to death, but the Israeli Supreme Court decided, despite the witness testimony, Demjanjuk had only been proven to be a guard, not "Ivan the Terrible." They freed him and ordered that he be deported to Ukraine, his native land.

Commercial Crimes

The U.S. criminologist Edwin Sutherland coined the term "white-collar crime" in 1939. He defined it as "crime committed by a person of respectability and high social status in the course of his occupation."

Commercial crimes do land high-profile executives in prison. In the U.K. four executives with the Guinness drinks company were jailed in 1990 for attempts to manipulate the stock market. A year later media tycoon Robert Maxwell's death saved him from a similar fate for embezzling staff pensions. Homemaking guru Martha Stewart was imprisoned in 2004 for insider trading, and by 2005 executives from the bankrupt U.S. energy corporation Enron were in jail for securities fraud. In 2007 two officials of Russia's bankrupt oil company, Yukos, were imprisoned for embezzling $13 billion.

Most crimes committed within businesses are, of course, on a smaller scale, but the average loss in the U.S.A. is $190,000. Embezzlement is among the most common and relatively easy to detect. Forensic investigators often trap embezzlers through forged signatures on checks and other recorded movements of money. In a Scottish case in 2006 Jackie Aitchenson was caught using Internet banking to embezzle £26,000 (about $50,000) from a medical center in Perthshire.

Opposite: Martha Stewart, America's homemaking advocate, departs Federal Court in New York City. She was convicted in 2004 of lying about a stock sale and received five months' imprisonment.

POSTAL FRAUD

Fraud is delivered straight into the home in the form of scams designed to obtain money, and these can frequently be traced back to the sender. They often appear in the form of a commercial misrepresentation such as get-rich-quick promises and work-at-home opportunities. Other illegal mailings include fraudulent charities and religious organizations soliciting donations. In some fraud cases merchandise that has been ordered and paid for is diverted on its way to the rightful owner. The latter, as well, has become a common type of Internet fraud.

Fake invoices are also a common scheme. In 2007 in Ontario, in Canada, the Toronto Police Service warned the public about letters being sent out claiming the recipient owed money in back taxes. The letters said payments by check could be made out to Stephen Smith at the Consumer Service Bureau. The police reminded the public that the government never asks for checks payable to an individual.

Former Enron Chief Executive Jeff Skilling (center) arrives at a courtroom in Houston, Texas, in 2006. He was found guilty of corporate fraud and received 24 years in prison.

Homemaking guru Martha Stewart was imprisoned in 2004 for insider trading.

CLUES TO FRAUD

Forensic scientists play a key role in investigating business fraud. They often detect it by examining questioned documents and identifying handwriting and signatures. According to a report by Britain's Forensic Science Service, a document examiner can reveal altered documents, fake identities, and false bank accounts by using chemical tests, specialized lighting, and the enhancement of hidden entries. The sequence of documents can also disclose a history of events in an illegal business transaction.

Forensic tests, including DNA profiles, can link suspects to documents, computers, and other office equipment. Valuable information can also be recovered from office security cameras, office computers, PDA palmtop computers, and cell phones, including cell site analyzes.

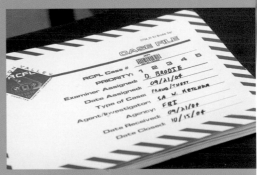

This file is at the computer forensics lab in Menlo Park, California, where fraud and other crimes are investigated.

Computer Crimes

The digital age has created the new field of computer crime, known as cyber crime. This immediately gave rise to computer forensic science, one of the fastest-growing disciplines within law enforcement.

The new forensic experts specialize in digital data used for an array of criminal activities, including hacking, identity theft, fraud, embezzlement, terrorism, software piracy, computer viruses, and child pornography.

DELETED FILES?

The ease of accessing computer files contributes to crime—but also to investigating it. Investigators can read "deleted" files recovered from a hard disk. They also can find deleted emails, hidden files and

TERRORISTS AND THE INTERNET

The Internet has become a major weapon for Islamic terrorist organizations such as al Qaeda. They use emails and coded messages to create a community of believers, send news of upcoming plans, and spread fear through images of beheadings and bombings. For their part, government agencies maintain constant efforts to take down these websites, although terrorists are often one step ahead, moving to new ones. Still, police forensic experts have had impressive successes. In 2004 they picked up leads on a website that showed the execution of an American victim, Paul Johnson, and traced the clues to Abdel Azziz al-Muqrin, the former top operative of al Qaeda in Saudi Arabia, who was then killed.

Paul Johnson (left) was a U.S. helicopter engineer in Saudi Arabia. His beheading by a group led by Abdel Azziz al-Muqrin (right) was shown on an Islamic website.

folders, Internet activity, and stolen data. Such services are available from the U.K.'s Forensic Science Service, whose eForensic Solutions portfolio includes cell-phone examinations. In the U.S.A., the FBI has a Computer Analysis and Response Team that coordinates its efforts with the Department of Defense Computer Forensic Laboratory. When forensic experts dismantle and examine computers that have been seized, they must photograph and note each part before investigating data on the hard disk. This documentation is needed to prove that the evidence was not contaminated.

UNTRACEABLE

One area in which investigators have been hindered by the switch from typewriters to computers is in tracing the source of a false document. Whereas each typewriter's letters had distinctive characteristics that could be read like its fingerprints, most computers use the same word-processing software, which is indistinguishable.

This computer equipment was taken as evidence on January 7, 2005 into the Silicon Valley Regional Computer Forensics Laboratory in Menlo Park, California.

Investigating the murder of wealthy American banker Robert Kissel in Hong Kong in 2003, a forensic computer specialist was aided by spyware Kissel had secretly installed on his wife's laptop. Nancy Kissel, also an American, was charged with serving her husband a milkshake laced with sedatives and then beating him to death.

Police officer Cheung Chun-kit found emails to the woman's lover and evidence she had searched the Internet for "Sleeping Pills," "Overdose Medication Causing Heart Attack," and "Drug Overdose." This evidence was combined with the discovery of her fingerprints on boxes of bloodstained clothes and bedding. She confessed, claiming in her defense that Kissel physically abused her, but in 2005 she was sentenced to life.

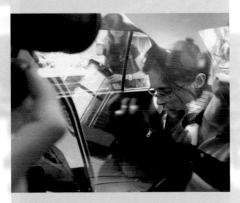

Nancy Kissel is surrounded by photographers as she leaves the High Court in Hong Kong on August 3, 2005.

Identity Fraud

Identity fraud costs the UK economy £1.7 billion ($3.35 billion) each year according to an estimate in 2006, about A$1.3 billion in Australia, and an estimated $55 billion in the U.S.A., the main victim.

INSTANT CREDIT, INSTANT IDENTITY THEFT

Bob Sullivan is one of America's leading journalists covering identity theft, having written the book, *Your Evil Twin: Behind the Identity Theft Epidemic* (2004), and more than 100 articles since 1996.

A prime reason for U.S. identity fraud, he says, is instant credit. "U.S. retailers waste no time throwing credit at anyone browsing high-ticket items in their stores," he notes. "Imposters can get their hands on valuable plastic with as little as a Social Security number and a name." And Sullivan knows the result: "Just as consumers can drive off a car lot in an hour with a brand new $30,000 car, so can their imposters."

Stealing personal information normally comes from the theft of a person's letters, credit cards, or checkbooks. Even documents thrown out with the garbage such as bills, receipts, and bank statements, can be used to steal someone's identity. A person who steals another's identity can use it to open bank accounts, withdraw funds from existing accounts, and apply for credit cards, loans, state benefits, and documents such as passports and driver's licenses. At worst, stolen

Holograms on a Chinese ID card help prevent counterfeiting. The color changes with the viewing angle, so normal copying fails.

false identities are used in the commission of crimes, which can include terrorism.

PHISHING

Emails are used to trick people into giving out bank personal identification numbers, computer passwords, and security numbers. Criminals use a technique known as "phishing" in which they pretend to be financial institutions or companies and send spam or pop-up messages requesting personal information.

More electronic identity theft comes from devices hidden in cash machines and card swipe machines. These skim details from the magnetic strip, while miniature cameras embedded in cash machines can record personal identification numbers.

FBI Cyber Division Assistant Director Jana Monroe unveils in 2004 in Los Angeles, California, an anti-piracy seal and warning text to be placed on digital and software intellectual property.

The FBI usually has more than 1600 active cases of identity theft being investigated at any one time. Its Cyber Division looks at such theft occurring over the Internet or through computer hacking. Forensic analysts review suspicious activity to identify and target those criminal organizations engaged in identity theft. They use a search engine called Choicepoint, which can provide the criminal's social security number and the names of potential family relatives and partners, along with addresses.

Nearly 30,000 phishing attacks were reported in January 2007 to the Anti-Phishing Working Group.

IDENTIFYING THE IDENTITY THIEF

Forensic scientists, especially forensic accountants, have ways of tracking identity thieves:

- If the thief uses a stolen credit card in a shop that has surveillance cameras, his or her image may have been captured and can be retrieved by checking the time of purchase on the invoice.

- If the perpetrator receives fraudulent checks, credit cards, or merchandise in the mail, the postal authorities may help to identify them.

- When a credit card is applied for under a false name, discrepancies can sometimes be seen in other information provided such as employment history or addresses.

Arson

Arson is considered to be a white-collar crime when the perpetrator sets a fire for financial gain, usually to collect insurance or to destroy company records. Financial arson is a serious crime that could accidentally kill.

The malicious setting of fires in the U.K. now averages 2100 incidents each week.

THE MIND OF AN ARSONIST

Australian psychologist Rebecca Doley has studied serial arsonists for more than ten years, interviewing more than 140 offenders. She says they receive more enjoyment from the aftermath than from the fire itself. Staying to watch the chaos they have caused gives the arsonists a sense of power. The fear of being caught does not act as a deterrent, she noted. "They understand what they are doing and the consequences of their actions, yet they choose to do it anyway."

The malicious setting of fires in the U.K. now averages 2,100 incidents each week, including arson attacks on cars, and the last decade has seen 2.4 million recorded arson fires. The annual cost is estimated to be some £3 billion ($6 billion). In recent years the U.S.A. has annually recorded more than 63,000 arson offences with an average damage of $356,324 to industrial and manufacturing buildings. About 4000 people are killed and 20,000 injured by arson attacks each year in the U.S.A.

Although most evidence would seem to be destroyed by fire, several clues can point investigators toward arson. Finding the "seat" of a fire, or its point of origin, can reveal how it started and spread. Accidental fires spread upward, creating a "V" shape pointing down to its origin. Fire started deliberately may have several "Vs" where an arsonist began separate fires. These may travel unnaturally across a floor, which indicates accelerants such as gasoline, or paint thinners were used. An accelerant that does not burn will leave an odor, and liquid accelerants create pool marks on the floor.

Arson investigators search burned debris in a similar way to forensic examiners working through a crime scene. They identify and collect evidence, preserving it carefully for laboratory tests and court proceedings. They wear protective clothing, and their tools include

Firefighters search carefully through the debris of a burned house. Evidence that is collected from the scene can help distinguish arson from an accident.

digital and video cameras, notebooks and pens, knives, screwdrivers, hammers, crowbars, evidence tags and tape, and evidence containers.

A family often loses everything they own in a malicious arson attack.

ABORIGINAL FIRESETTING

It may seem like arson to some, but the practice of setting fires by Australian Aboriginals is not classified as such by the Australian government. These natives, who arrived in Australia some 50,000 years ago, were using fire for land management long before Europeans settlers arrived. The importance of these fires is evident by the different names the Aboriginals give to various types. Aboriginal peoples continue to light fires even when new agricultural practices mean that they are no longer needed or desirable. In some cases the fires can cause property damage or livestock losses. The Australian government considers this fire-setting not malicious in nature, since the bush is not set alight to destroy or damage property. It is therefore not classified as arson, excluding some Aboriginal people who might be guilty of traditional arson.

Counterfeit Money

Currency counterfeiting for financial gain and to destabilize economies is an ancient crime. The U.S. dollar, the currency most used for global transactions, is copied the most.

Computers makes it possible for unskilled operators to produce excellent color reproductions.

HOW TO DETECT COUNTERFEIT MONEY

Here are some general tips on how to examine money to identify counterfeit notes. On genuine currency:

- Serial numbers are evenly spaced and have a distinctive style.
- Fine lines on the borders are clear and unbroken.
- Some lines and other printing is embedded. Counterfeit notes have printing on top of the paper.

Used worldwide, the dollar is the main victim of counterfeiters.

Left: An operator uses the RAPACE system to help detect counterfeit Euros. The system allows the operator and enquirer to communicate by telephone.

Below: Special fluorescent ink and strips glow bright blue and red under ultraviolet light to show this is a genuine Euro banknote.

In 2006 some 50,000 euro notes were counterfeited each month. Forty-four percent of the counterfeit copies were 20-euro notes and a further 36 percent were 50-euro notes. The Forgery of Money unit of Europol, the European Police force, maintains a database on counterfeiters and another monitors the technical aspects of reproducing currency.

The problem has multiplied with the advent of easily available high-resolution printers and copiers. Computer-generated counterfeiting makes it possible for unskilled operators to produce excellent color reproductions. Forensic examination, however, can detect the printed image resting on top of the paper's surface and, under a low-grade magnification of about 20x, small particles of toner can often be seen outside the image area.

National currencies, as well, have special protective marks such a micro printing and built-in ultraviolet features. A silver foil strip is embedded inside U.K. paper currency, U.S. currency has tiny red and blue fibers embedded throughout, Canadian notes have a holographic strip, and Australia now produces only polymer notes with a plastic substrate.

RUSSIAN COUNTERFEITERS LIKE THE EURO

Counterfeiters in Russia are switching from the dollar to the euro, it was announced in March 2007 by Alexander Prokopchuk, deputy head of Interpol's National Central Bureau at the Russian Interior Ministry. He said that from 2005 to 2006 the number of confiscated counterfeit banknotes rose from 979 to 1138. The new banknote total was worth €106,440. Prokopchuk also noted that the number of counterfeit ruble notes had risen 60.6 percent in a year, with 118,000 notes worth more than 104 million rubles confiscated in 2006. This is despite the introduction in 2004 by the Russian Central Bank of notes "which would be impossible to fabricate at least during the coming seven years." The new rubles contain a watered silk stripe filled with thin parallel lines. If it is turned, the one-colour stripe will become multicoloured with yellow, pink, and blue stripes. The new notes follow a recommendation by Interpol that all countries introduce new modified notes every five or seven years, since criminal gangs learn to make high-quality counterfeit notes in that period of time.

Document Forgeries

It is easy to produce an accurate-looking copy of any document, but forgers tend to target those involving identity such as passports, and papers regarding money, including wills.

Experts detect altered documents by using microscopes as well as oblique light, which can expose areas deleted with an eraser or correction fluid.

Examining the types of paper, ink, and glues used can discover the similarity of documents and their dating. Documents that have been printed or copied by modern machines can be analyzed for telltale marks such as those made by a laser printer's drum or a photocopier's glass.

HANDWRITING

Handwriting styles can be duplicated, but forensic-document examiners can see through skilful forgeries. They look at the shape of individual letters, paying special attention to their size and the way they are slanted and connected. They also check for inconsistencies of spelling, preferred characters such as the use of "&" instead of "and," grammar, punctuation, and content. It was the latter that caught the American terrorist Unabomber in 1996 when his brother compared the content and word phrases in his published manifesto to writings he had left at home.

Even signatures and sample words can be exposed as fakes. When the two-year-old son of aviator Charles Lindbergh was kidnapped and murdered, a comparison of letters in the ransom note with the signature of Bruno Hauptmann confirmed that he was the perpetrator.

Other clues to forged writing include pen lifts at odd places where the forger was checking his writing, and any retouching of the script. If tracing has been done, a heavy indentation may be visible, or the bottom original may leave evidence on the paper put over it.

FISH

The U.S. Secret Service and Germany's Bundeskriminalamt use FISH (the Forensic Information System for Handwriting). This system, based on work carried out by German law enforcement in the 1980s, has now cataloged the handwriting of more than 100,000 individuals and found no two people with the same combinations of handwriting characteristics. FISH scans a block of text and plots the handwriting as arithmetic and geometric values.

James Sellers shows the similarity of Bruno Hauptmann's signature with individual letters on the ransom note. Sellers testified at Hauptmann's trial.

Left: Time *magazine was among the world media that covered the exposure of the Hitler Diaries as fakes. Amazingly, the volumes were first judged to be legitimate by three document experts.*

Right: *A sample page from the Hitler Diaries. They were made on modern paper using modern ink, but some historians were still fooled.*

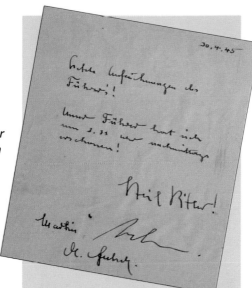

HITLER DIARIES

The German magazine *Stern* paid nine million marks in 1981 to purchase diaries that were supposedly written by Adolf Hitler. Three independent document examiners compared the diaries' handwriting with Hitler's, and came to the conclusion that they matched. However, the publishers asked the Federal Institute of Forensic Investigation in Berlin to examine them. The paper and inks proved they were fraudulent, because the bindings, and a substance used to whiten the paper, had not been invented until after Hitler's death. Tests showed the ink in one section was not even a year old when examined. The forger, Konrad Kujau, and his middleman, *Stern* reporter Gerd Heidemann, were each sentenced to four and a half years in prison.

Art Forgeries

The production of fake art has long been a lucrative business. Superficially, forged art "masterpieces" are difficult to discern, even by some gallery, museum, and auction experts.

Many cases can only be solved by forensic analyses that look at the age of a painting and compare it with other genuine pieces by the same artist.

Cracking the surface paint with varnish or rolling the canvas often ages a fake painting. A stereo-microscope can detect this more recent effort, and X-rays will reveal if the cracking reaches each paint level. Ultra-violet radiation can determine the age of a varnish and also reveal any sketching, retouching, and painted-over areas.

X-RAYS

The type of pigments used can also help dating, since the years they were introduced are known. The modern chrome yellow pigment, for example, can be identified by a scanning electron microscope (SEM), because the modern version has been coated for the past 30 years to protect it from pollution that once turned it black.

Ceramic artworks are difficult to copy, and experts use thermo-luminescence to date them, since it measures the radiation the clay has absorbed since it was fired. Copies of metal figures are easy to cast, but an SEM can differentiate metals used today from older ones. X-ray fluorescence will date metal pieces because they emit an X-ray spectrum of the alloy used to make it.

Right: A forgery of a painting by Lucas Cranach the Elder is exposed by ultraviolet light which causes it to fluoresce. The dark areas were retouched.

Above: A technician at the Doerner Institute in Munich, Germany operates the infrared scanner that found the forged painting supposedly by Lucas Cranach the Elder.

LASERS AND CERAMICS

A forensic scientist in Perth, Australia, is using lasers to trace pottery back to its kiln site to expose ceramic forgeries. Emma Bartle from the Center for Forensic Science at the University of Western Australia developed the scientific method to authenticate porcelain.

Bartle said forged Chinese Ming and Japanese Imari porcelain is a multimillion-dollar industry in South-east Asia. "These modern fakes are so detailed and sophisticated," she noted, "that gone are the days whereby trained experts can authenticate pieces using visual examination alone."

The lasers analyze the porcelain's chemical composition to trace its origins back to production in China or Japan. "Each site has a different combination of trace elements such as strontium and lanthanum, which is unique," she said.

Ultra-violet radiation can determine the age of a varnish and reveal retouching.

COMPUTER ANALYSIS

Professor Hany Farid and his colleagues at Dartmouth College in Hanover, New Hampshire, have developed a computer tool for analyzing digital images to detect art forgeries. Announced in 2004, the technique classifies paintings and drawings by a digital analysis of an artist's style. High-resolution digital scans break down an image into "wavelets." These are simple elements and can be analyzed by a complex mathematical model to check for consistencies between works of art or within a single one.

When applied to 13 drawings, the technique automatically grouped the 8 real works of the sixteenth-century Flemish artist Pieter Bruegel the Elder, separating them from 5 modern copies.

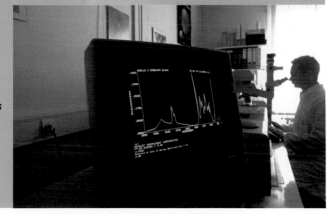

A popular method for detecting art forgeries is by using a spectrophotometer that can reveal the type of resin in the paint.

Fake Products

Throughout the world, the manufacture and sale of fake products has become an immense industry estimated to represent up to seven percent of world trade.

Above: Nestle CEO Peter Brabeck-Latmathe at the 2007 meeting of the Business Action to Stop Counterfeiting and Piracy in Geneva, Switzerland.

Right: Michel Danet, secretary general of the World Customs Organization, displays fake goods in 2004 in Brussels at the global congress on combating counterfeiting.

Main Picture: A policeman adds fake and pirate software disks to the large pile to be destroyed at a factory in Xian in Shaanxi Province, China, in 2005. Police destroyed more than 100,000 confiscated disks during the operation.

The FBI estimates that this illegal trade costs Americans about $250 billion a year, and other research found some 750,000 U.S. jobs have been lost to fake products.

Michel Danet, the secretary general of the World Customs Organization, warns that the production of fake products is a serious criminal offence and should be considered as an act of economic sabotage.

COUNTERFEIT

It can be extremely difficult to distinguish between genuine and counterfeit products. As well, almost any item has been illegally copied, from doorknobs and shoe polish to food, drugs, watches, cigarettes, clothing, electronic equipment, perfume, and even airplane engines. Worldwide research in 80 countries in 2005 by the Business Action to Stop Counterfeiting and Piracy (BASCAP), part of the International Chamber of Commerce located in Paris, found that 40 percent of counterfeited brands involve software giants, clothes designers, pharmaceutical companies, printer manufacturers, and luxury goods retailers.

SUPPORTING CRIME

"In some counterfeit goods the quality is so good that it really takes a forensic expert to tell if it's fake or not," says Michelle Moore, a spokeswoman for the International Anti-Counterfeiting Coalition (IACC). She adds, "And even though these places may look like innocent mom-and-pop shops, they're often connected to organized-crime rings."

The IACC, located in Washington, D.C., points out that counterfeiters do not pay taxes or fair wages and often use forced child labor. The profits have also been linked to organized crime, drug trafficking, and terrorist activity. "When you purchase a fake," it warned, "you become part of the cycle of counterfeiting and your money directly supports these things you would never want to support."

CUSTOMS

Every country is facing a nightmare battle. In 2007 India had 44 fake versions of Vicks VapoRub. In Malta during the first two months of 2007, customs officials intercepted over half a million counterfeit products. In Virginia police raided 11 Newport News stores, and found that 90 percent of the goods were fakes.

The quality of some counterfeit goods is so high that it really takes a forensic expert to tell if it's fake or not.

RECOGNIZING FAKES

Each type of product (diamonds, pearls, designer bags, etc.) has been counterfeited in a different way, so it is impossible to list specific advice on detecting a fake. Consumers can follow a few general rules to educate themselves, and Ed Kelly, an intellectual property rights attorney in Thailand, says shoppers should keep the "Three Ps" in mind:

- **Package:** Look at the quality of the product and its packaging. Watch for things such as poor stitching or incorrectly spelled brand names or logos.

- **Price:** If the price is too good to be true, it probably is.

- **Place:** Brand name products are sold in shops or through the official company website, not on the streets or open-air markets.

Psychological Profiling

Perpetrators of crimes, especially those driven by compulsions, will normally commit a series of crimes in a similar manner—a phenomenon which can be exploited by the forensic psychologist.

Psychological profiling, also known as criminal or offender profiling, is done in two different ways. In one the assumption is made that a criminal such as a serial killer will behave as other similar criminals have in the past. It may thus be decided that a pedophile may use teenage Internet chatrooms to contact a victim and arrange a meeting.

The other way of profiling is to study the habits, or *modus operandi* (method of operating) of one criminal who repeatedly commits a crime instead of generalizing he or she is like others. A rapist may be extremely organized such as making appointments with real estate dealers at unoccupied houses, or may have a "signature" habit such as mutilating the victim. A profiler who combines the two methods should have a better understanding of the characteristics of an offender.

Carine Hutsebaut is a psychotherapist at the International Centre for Molested and Abducted Children in Brussels, Belgium. She specializes in pedophile psychology.

Investigators also profile victims, in a process known as "victimology." Gaining an understanding of why they are selected at a particular place or time can lead investigators to the criminal. If several prostitutes are killed, the murderer may be a customer or may even be a fanatical moralist.

Profiling grew out of studies made by the FBI. The bureau's Behavioral Analysis Unit has put together reports profiling types of criminals, such as child abductors and those who go on killing sprees in schools.

Police detectives question a man after the murder of Maartje Tamboezer near a railroad station in Surrey, England. The 1986 case saw Britain's first use of psychological offender profiling that led to John Duffy's conviction.

SIGNATURES

A criminal's signature is derived from his psychological needs and fantasies. Whereas such *modus operandi* as wearing a disguise or a particular way of lying in wait for a victim is a method of committing a crime, a signature is a criminal's personal, superfluous addition or "calling card," which has nothing to do with pulling off a crime. Examples of signatures include torture, arranging the corpse in a certain way, and taking souvenirs.

RACIAL PROFILING

One danger of police profiling is discriminatory racial profiling. Muslims have complained in Britain about being stopped in airports for special checks. More common are routine stop-and-search procedures that, for example, can happen to Hispanics in the south-western U.S.A. more often than to white people. Black people in Canada even have a name for these checks, called "DWB" for "driving while black."

Some such as Haras Rafiq, spokesman for the Sufi Muslim Council in Britain, accept the reality of profiling. "I regularly get checked, double-checked, and sometimes triple checked," he noted in 2007. "I get asked the same questions again and again. I understand the reason why they have to do this, and passengers need to be mindful and understand this as well."

A "Redeem the Dream" march on Washington, D.C., in 2000 focused on racial profiling and police brutality.

Gaining an understanding of why a victim was selected at a particular place or time can lead investigators to the criminal.

The Forensic Psychiatrist

A forensic psychiatrist evaluates a suspect or indicted person to determine his or her personality, intelligence, and mental competency to stand trial.

In cases of a false confession the person may have psychiatric problems or be manipulative, trying to deflect interest from a more serious crime, or just trying to acquire some sort of fame. No reason was discovered when John Mark Karr confessed in 2006 to killing the six-year-old American beauty queen JonBenet Ramsey in 1996 in Boulder, Colorado.

Forensic psychiatrists Dr. Henry Kennedy and Dr. Sarah Henley were part of the 1999 London trial of Louise Sullivan, the nanny given a suspended sentence for the manslaughter of a child.

A test for "competency to stand trial," as it is known in the U.S.A., is important because a suspect with real mental problems such as delusions or paranoia will be unable to understand the court processes or even what he or she is charged with. British courts are more likely to detain such people in hospitals instead of prisons.

MENTAL DISORDER

Suspects may also be ruled incompetent if they have a severe alcohol or drug problem. Psychiatrists look out for criminals feigning a mental disorder with the intention of entering a plea of insanity.

A possible finding in Canadian courts would be "not criminally responsible on account of mental disorder." A common plea in the U.S.A. is "diminished capacity," which says some conditions altered a perpetrator's ability to distinguish between right and wrong, as when a person in an uncontrollable fit of rage kills another.

RORSCHACH TESTS

Besides interviewing a suspect, a forensic psychiatrist can use tests.

One such test involves asking the suspect what images he sees in the abstract inkblots of the Rorschach test, and what stories he can create from pictures in the Thematic Apperception Test (TAT).

RUDOLPH HESS

One of the most famous cases of unfitness to plead occurred at the Nuremberg trial of Rudolf Hess, the Nazi Deputy-Führer who had been declared insane by Hitler. Hess flew secretly to Scotland apparently to arrange a peace treaty. Parachuting from his Messerschmitt, he was quickly arrested. While imprisoned in Britain, he displayed signs of mental instability to his British captors.

At his trial Hess talked to himself, laughed for no obvious reason, and counted on his fingers. Psychiatrists who examined him were not quite sure he was mentally ill but decided he was unfit to plead because he was not mentally capable of following the proceedings to defend himself. Despite this, Hess was imprisoned at Spandau Prison in West Berlin and, in 1987 at the age of 93, committed suicide.

Above: Rudolph Hess (front row, second left) sits through long testimonies at the Nuremberg trials. He is flanked by two other infamous Nazis, Hermann Goering on his right and Joachim von Ribbentrop on his left.

CONFIDENTIALITY

The psychiatrist-patient rule of confidentiality is endangered by the needs of the legal process. If limitations are placed on confidentiality, the forensic psychiatrist should make the suspect aware of these. While an assessment will be made of the suspect's mental state, the detailed information received in the interview should be kept as confidential.

Left: A forensic psychiatrist (right) lends support to a relative of 1 of the 18 passengers killed in a bus fire on October 23, 2006 in Panama City, Panama. The fire was caused by mechanical problems.

The Polygraph

The polygraph, or lie detector, has had an unusual effect on criminal justice. Some suspects have refused to take it, thereby raising suspicions, while others have taken the chance and been proven liars.

There is no doubt that an unemotional murderer might cheat it, and a totally innocent person could panic on crucial questions and send readings awry.

This is why the instrument is seldom used as evidence in the courtroom. Yet the FBI gives about 8,000 tests each year, reacting to the arrest in 2001 of Robert Hanssen, who never underwent one in 25 years at the bureau and was found to be a Russian spy. The CIA also administers tests to help stop employees from leaking information,

and other U.S. agencies now use them more than ever.

In July 2007 the U.K. government introduced polygraph testing of sex offenders on licence from a sentence of imprisonment of 12 months or more, a practise that is already established in the U.S.A.

STRESS LEVELS

A polygraph measures a person's stress level through a progression of questions. Electrodes on the suspect's fingers can detect the lower electrical resistance in the

skin which is caused by increased perspiration. A sphygmomanometer cuff around the arm also measures an increased pulse, and two pneumographs strapped around the chest measure heavy breathing caused by anxiety. The data is fed into a computer that produces a graph, a digital replacement for the old needle that used to scribble lines over a scrolling paper. The examiner starts by asking innocent questions to create a baseline of truthfulness for the purposes of comparison.

WHO INVENTED THE POLYGRAPH?

William Moulton Marston has often been credited with the invention of a simple polygraph in 1917, which measured blood pressure. His doctoral thesis at Harvard University in 1921 was "Systolic blood pressure symptoms of deception and constituent mental states." This was ironic because Marston also created the comic character Wonder Woman who roped evil-doers with her golden lariat, which made them tell the truth.
It was John A. Larson, the first U.S. policeman with a Ph.D., who devised the polygraph known today. He added measurements for heart rate, respiration, and skin conductivity. This was also in 1921, while he was a student at the University of California, and he first tested it on female students.

A U.S. murder suspect takes a lie detector test on November 17, 1926 when it was known as a "truth detector test." Like a polygraph, this early verson of the sphygmomanometer measured changes in blood pressure.

Right: A woman undergoes a polygraph test as part of her application to work at the FBI headquarters in Quantico, Virginia, U.S.A. All new recruits must take a lie-detector test.

Below: Pulse meters are attached to a man's fingers for a polygraph test. The meters measure his heart rate, and under the subject's hands are the traces produced by the polygraph. These results are combined with measurements of blood pressure and respiration rate.

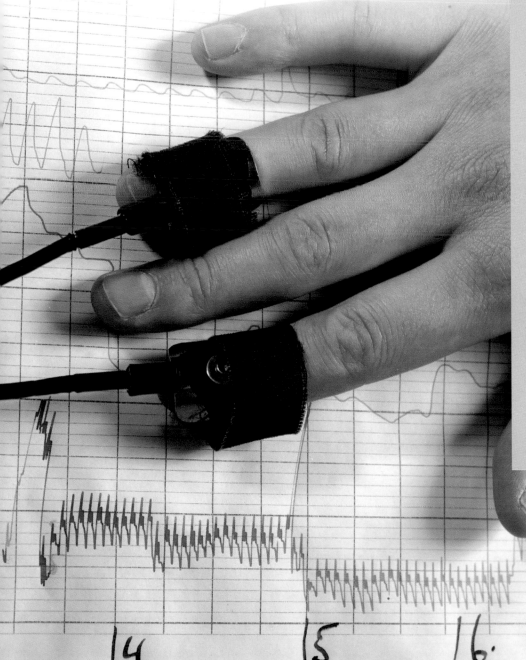

TWO U.S. VIEWS

"The physiological responses measured by the polygraph are not uniquely related to deception. That is, the responses measured by the polygraph do not all reflect a single underlying process: a variety of psychological and physiological processes, including some that can be consciously controlled, can affect polygraph measures and tests." – *National Research Council, 2003*

"What is not subject to debate and appears to be beyond dispute is that the polygraph does not detect lies." – *U.S. Congressional Research Service, 2007*

STOELTING CO.   CHICAGO, ILL., U.S.A.   CAT. NO. 25935   MADE IN U.

Electroencephalograph

If the polygraph has its doubters, the electroencephalograph (EEG) has few. It has been used since the 1930s to track electrical waves coursing through our brains.

Computer-based "Brain Fingerprinting," invented in the U.S.A. by Dr. Lawrence A. Farwell (*see box*), uses the Memory and Encoding Related Multifaceted Electroencephalographic Response (MERMER). This is a brain reaction that kicks in when a person recognizes something of personal significance.

An electrical signal, known as P300, surges from the brain about 300 milliseconds after it confronts a significant image such as a victim's face. This does not depend on the emotions of the suspect, only information stored in the brain. There is no testing to see if the suspect is telling the truth. The test can only indicate if he or she has certain information stored in their brain.

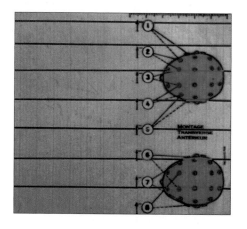

A colored electroencephalograph (EEG) indicates a brain death. The eight brainwaves are flat because there are no electrical impulses being produced by the brain.

BRAIN FINGERPRINTING

In a Brain Fingerprinting test, a suspect wears a headband with electronic sensors that measure the EEG from several locations on the scalp. He or she is shown images, words, and phrases on a computer screen, some innocent and some connected to a crime. Brain Fingerprinting thus matches evidence at the crime scene with evidence in the brain.

The innocent images are used to establish the baseline response. The brain wave alters when an image is recognized, and guilty suspects cannot suppress their reaction as they can with a polygraph. A computer is then used to analyze the reaction.

Innocent suspects have no MERMER when, for example, they are shown a crime scene they do not know. In tests run on FBI and CIA agents, Brain Fingerprinting proved one hundred percent accurate. In the FBI test 17 agents were separated from four non-agents by displaying images that only the FBI agents would recognize.

A MERMER CONVICTION

Brain Fingerprinting was instrumental in obtaining a confession and guilty plea from serial killer James Grinder in 1999 in Missouri. Dr. Farwell gave the test to Grinder, showing him images connected to an unsolved murder, and the suspect's brain reaction confirmed a match. Grinder pled guilty to the rape and murder of Julie Helton and was given a life sentence without parole. He has since also confessed to killing three other women.

DR. LAWRENCE A. FARWELL

The inventor of Brain Fingerprinting technology, Lawrence A. Farwell, is a former research associate at Harvard University. He is now the chairman and chief scientist of the Brain Fingerprinting Laboratories in Seattle, Washington. He also invented the Farwell Brain Communicator. This allows a paralyzed person to communicate directly to a computer and speech synthesizer using electrical brain activity.

Dr. Farwell also has undertaken research that demonstrates the direct effect of human consciousness on matter at the quantum-mechanical level. As a result of his work he wrote the book *How Consciousness Commands Matter: The New Scientific Revolution and the Evidence that Anything Is Possible* (2001).

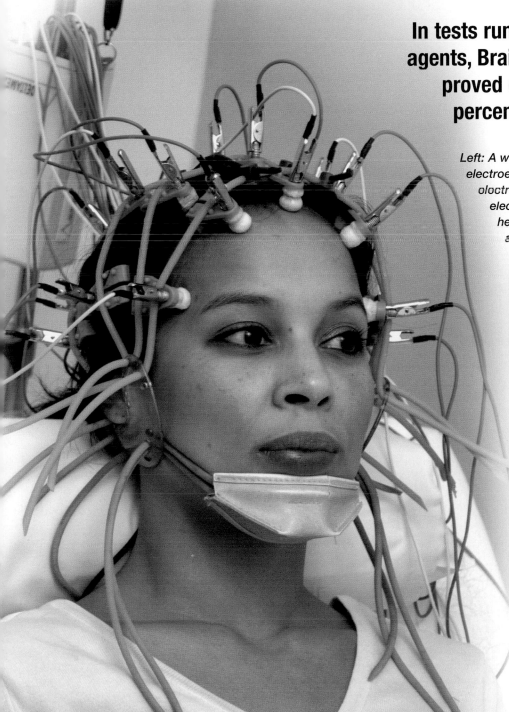

In tests run on FBI and CIA agents, Brain Fingerprinting proved one hundred percent accurate.

Left: A woman undergoes an electroencephalograph. The numerous electrodes attached to her head record the electrical activity from different parts of her brain as it reacts to external visual or auditory stimuli.

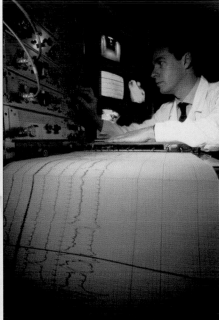

Above: A routine check is made of an EEG machine which is recording a subject's brain activity by producing a printout with the characteristic wave patterns.

Criminal Insanity

"Not guilty by reason of insanity" is a shaky defense that covers various mental states. The law believes a criminal cannot be held responsible for his or her actions if that person has no perception of reality.

Other definitions include whether or not the person could tell right from wrong, whether they could control their behavior and if they intended to act the way they did.

Forensic psychiatrists and psychologists know that it is not easy to explain the mind of the criminal within these terms. Many with mental health problems do know right from wrong, have a grasp on reality, are not subject to irresistible urges, and can anticipate the results of their actions.

When ordinary neighbors commit insane crimes, they are often living in their own realities. A loving mother smothers her children to save them from the wicked world, or a reliable coworker turns out to be a schizoid serial killer.

If a disturbed or mentally ill person commits a crime but lives in our reality, courts will often find them criminally responsible. In the U.S.A., this may land them on death row. Several prisoners described as "mentally retarded" have been executed, but the U.S. Supreme Court ruled in 2002 that executing retarded prisoners violated the Constitution's protection against "cruel and unusual punishments."

Psychiatrists have pointed out other differences in the minds of violent offenders. Some have a distinctive lack of empathy for their victims, some are unable to control their behavior and others have predisposing factors such as a father's history of violence.

SON OF SAM

David Berkowitz, nicknamed "Son of Sam," was a serial killer who terrorized New York City in the 1970s. He wrote a strange letter to the police saying he was the "Son of Sam" and "Papa Sam keeps me locked in the attic too." He was eventually caught in 1977 after receiving a parking ticket close to the scene of his latest murder. A search of his car revealed the gun. Berkowitz said that howling dogs in the neighborhood were possessed by ancient demons that ordered him to go out and kill. This suggested a plea of insanity, but he confessed to killing six people and in 1978 received six life sentences.

David Berkowitz arrives at the Brooklyn Criminal Courts Building after his arrest on August 10, 1977 outside his Yonkers, New York, home.

Right: U.S. Attorney Wendell Odom delivers his closing arguments in the second murder trial of his client Andrea Yates, in which she was found not guilty of murder by reason of insanity.

SATAN WITHIN

Andrea Yates drowned her five children one by one in the bath in 2001 in the area of Houston, Texas. At her second trial in 2006, she was found not guilty by reason of insanity after the jury was told she suffered from severe postpartum psychosis, and in a delusional state believed Satan was inside her. She said she was trying to save her children from hell. An earlier sentence of guilt was overturned, and Yates was sentenced to a mental hospital.

Yates and her lawyers George Parnham (left) and Wendell Odom react to the new verdict in 2006.

If a disturbed or mentally ill person commits a crime but lives in our reality, courts will often find them criminally responsible.

Texas Penal Code § 8.01. Insanity

a) It is an affirmative defense to p that, at the time of the condu actor, **as a result of severe** disease or defect, did not kn conduct was wrong

Index